# SOUPS
### AND
# STARTERS

# 366
## RECIPES

# SOUPS
## AND
# STARTERS

SUNBURST BOOKS

This edition first published in 1994 by
Sunburst Books, Deacon House, 65 Old Church Street,
London, SW3 5BS.

Copyright © 1994 Sunburst Books

ISBN 1 85778 059 0

Printed and bound in India

# CONTENTS

# HOT SOUPS

## SALMON VICHYSSOISE
### Serves 4

*2 oz (50 g) butter*
*1 lb (450 g) leeks, cleaned, trimmed and finely chopped*
*8 oz (225 g) onions, finely chopped*
*1 pt (600 ml) fish or chicken stock*
*15 oz (425 g) can pink salmon, drained, boned and flaked (reserve juice)*
*8 oz (225 g) potatoes, peeled and chopped*
*salt and freshly ground black pepper*
*1/2 pt (300 ml) milk*

Melt the butter in a large pan. Add the leeks and onion and cook very gently until they soften. Pour in the stock and reserved fish juice, add the potatoes and seasoning, then cover and leave to simmer for 20 minutes, stirring occasionally, until the potatoes are tender. Pour the soup into a blender or food processor and liquidise until almost smooth. Return to the pan, then add the milk and salmon. Heat until bubbling. Adjust the seasoning and serve.

## FRESH PEA SOUP
### Serves 4

*2 oz (50 g) butter*
*1 small onion, finely chopped*
*2 lb (900 g) fresh peas, shelled*
*2 pts (1.1 litres) chicken stock*
*1/2 tsp caster sugar*
*2 large sprigs fresh mint*
*salt and pepper*
*2 egg yolks (size 2)*
*5 fl oz (150 ml) double cream*
*fresh mint to garnish*

Sauté onion in melted butter until soft but not coloured. Add the peas and sauté for a few minutes. Add stock, sugar and sprigs of mint, bring to the boil and simmer for about 30 minutes or until peas are tender. Put soup through a fine sieve or puree in a blender. Add seasoning to taste and return to clean pan. Whisk egg yolks and cream together, add to the soup and heat gently, stirring to avoid curdling. Serve garnished with a sprig of fresh mint.

## AMERICAN CHOWDER
### Serves 4-6

*1 lb (450 g) cod fillet, skinned and cut into 3 or 4 pieces*
*4 rashers unsmoked back bacon, derinded and chopped*
*1 large onion, thinly sliced*
*1 oz (25 g) butter*
*2 medium potatoes, cut into cubes*
*1 pt (600 ml) milk*
*3 tbsp plain flour*
*1 bay leaf*
*2 oz (50 g) white crabmeat or chopped crabstick*
*11 oz (325 g) tin sweetcorn*
*salt and freshly ground black pepper*
*2 tsp lemon juice*
*croutons, for garnish*

Add the fish to about 1 pint (600 ml) simmering salted water and cook for 10 minutes. Drain the fish and remove any bones. Reserve ½ pt (300 ml) of the cooking liquid. Fry the bacon and onion in the butter in a large pan for about 5 minutes, add the potatoes and cook for a few more minutes. Add the reserved fish stock. Blend a little of the milk with the flour, stir into the pan with the remaining milk and the bay leaf. Bring to the boil and cook for 20 minutes until the potato is softening. Roughly flake in the fish and the crabmeat and also add the sweetcorn. Cook for a further 5 minutes. Season well and add the lemon juice. Serve accompanied by a bowl of crisp croutons.

## LETTUCE SOUP
### Serves 4

*2 oz (50 g) butter*
*12 oz (350 g) lettuce leaves*
*4 oz (110 g) spring onions, trimmed*
*1 level tbsp plain flour*
*1 pt (600 ml) chicken stock*
*¼ pt (150 ml) milk*
*salt and pepper*

Melt the butter in a deep saucepan and sauté the roughly chopped lettuce and spring onions until very soft. Stir in the flour and then add the stock. Bring to the boil, cover and simmer for 35 minutes. When cool, puree in a blender or rub through a sieve. Return to the saucepan and add the milk and seasoning. Reheat to serving temperature.

# CREAM OF CARROT AND LEMON SOUP
## Serves 6-8

*4oz (110 g) unsalted butter*
*1 large onion, chopped*
*1 large clove garlic, chopped*
*1½ lb (700g) carrots, peeled and sliced*
*3 tomatoes, chopped*
*1 baking potato, peeled and sliced*
*2 oz (50 g) fresh basil, shredded or flat leaved parsley*
*24 fl oz (720 ml) chicken stock*
*salt and freshly ground black pepper*
*6 fl oz (180 ml) crème fraîche*
*¼ tsp hot pepper sauce*
*2 fl oz (60 ml) lemon juice*
*carrot curls, crème fraîche and flat leaved parsley to garnish*

Melt 3 oz of the butter in a large saucepan, add the onion and garlic, cover the pan and cook gently over a low heat for about 5 minutes until softened but not browned. Add the carrots, tomatoes, potatoes, basil, stock, salt, pepper and remaining butter. Bring quickly to the boil, reduce the heat until simmering, cover the pan and cook for about 45 minutes until the vegetables are tender. Liquidise in a food processor or blender until smooth. Return to the pan and add the crème fraîche and the hot pepper sauce, simmering for a further 15 minutes uncovered. Just before serving stir in the lemon juice. Ladle into individual soup bowls and garnish each with a carrot curl, a spoonful of crème fraîche and a parsley sprig.

# CARROT SOUP
## Serves 4

*2 oz (50 g) butter*
*12 oz (350 g) carrots, peeled and diced or grated*
*2 leeks or onions, sliced*
*¾ pint (450 ml) chicken stock*
*salt and pepper*
*¼ pint (150 ml) milk*
*6 tbsp fresh single cream*
*chopped parsley to garnish*

Fry the carrots and leeks or onions in melted butter for 5-10 minutes. Add stock and seasoning and simmer for 15-20 minutes. Sieve or puree and return to the pan. Stir in the milk and fresh cream; adjust seasoning and heat, but do not boil. Serve sprinkled with parsley.

## CURRIED PARSNIP SOUP
### Serves 6

*1¹/₂ oz (35 g) butter*
*1 medium onion, sliced*
*1¹/₂ lb parsnips (675 g), peeled and finely diced*
*1 level tsp curry powder*
*¹/₂ tsp ground cumin*
*2¹/₂ pints (1.5 litres) chicken stock*
*salt and freshly ground pepper*
*5 fl oz (150 ml) single cream*
*paprika to garnish*

Heat the butter in the base of a large pan and fry the onion and parsnip for about 3 minutes. Stir in the curry powder and cumin and fry for 2 minutes. Add the stock, bring to the boil, reduce heat and simmer, covered, for about 5 minutes, until the vegetables are tender. Cool slightly, then use a perforated draining spoon to place the vegetables in a blender, add a little stock and puree until smooth. Return to the pan. Adjust seasoning, add the fresh cream and reheat to serving temperature but do not boil. Serve sprinkled with paprika.

## HARICOT BEAN SOUP
### Serves 4-6

*1 oz (25 g) butter*
*8 oz (225 g) onions, chopped*
*3 rashers streaky bacon*
*8 oz (225g) potatoes, diced*
*1 clove garlic, crushed*
*8 oz (225 g) haricot beans, soaked overnight*
*salt and white pepper*
*bouquet garni*
*3 pts (1.8 litres) vegetable or ham stock*
*¹/₄ pt (150 ml) cream*
*parsley, chopped*

Derind and chop the bacon and sauté gently in the butter with the onions and garlic for about 4 minutes, stirring to avoid browning. Then add the potatoes and drained beans and cook gently for another 10 minutes shaking the pan frequently. Add the seasoning, bouquet garni and stock. Stir well, bring to the boil, cover, and simmer for 2-3 hours or until the beans are cooked. Liquidise in a blender or rub through a sieve until smooth, return to the pan with the cream and reheat gently. Serve with croutons and chopped parsley.

# PEPPER SOUP
## Serves 4

*2 tbsp oil*
*2 oz (50 g) butter*
*1 red pepper*
*1 yellow pepper*
*2 onions, chopped*
*1¹/₂ oz (35 g) flour*
*³/₄ pt (450 ml) chicken stock*
*salt and pepper*
*³/₄ pt (450 ml) milk*
*3 tbsp single cream*

Grill the peppers until the skin is blistered and blackened, and remove the skins when the peppers are cool enough to handle. Remove the seeds and pith and then chop. Sauté the onion and garlic in the melted butter and oil for 5 minutes, add the chopped peppers and cook gently for a further 5 minutes. Add the flour, stirring, and cook for a minute, then pour in the stock, still stirring, until the soup thickens. Season, cover the pan and simmer for about 25 minutes, or until the vegetables are tender. Sieve or liquidise in a blender, rinse out the saucepan and return the soup to the pan with the milk. Gently reheat, adjust seasoning if necessary and stir in the cream just before serving.

# SPINACH AND ORANGE SOUP
## Serves 6-8

*4 oz (110g) butter*
*2¹/₄ lb (1 kg) fresh leaf spinach, cleaned, trimmed and roughly chopped*
*2 medium onions, finely chopped*
*2 oranges, juice and grated rind*
*4 level tbsp flour*
*1¹/₂ pints (900 ml) chicken stock*
*1¹/₂ pints (900 ml) milk*
*salt and black pepper*
*shreds of orange rind, blanched.*

Add the vegetables to the melted butter in a heavy-based pan with the grated orange rind (reserving a few strips). Cover with a piece of wet greaseproof paper and the lid, then sweat for about 25 minutes. Stir in the flour, stock and milk off the heat. Return to the heat, bring to the boil, season and simmer for 15 minutes. Puree the soup, then reheat for serving, adding the orange juice at the last minute. Garnish with the reserved orange rind.

# MULLIGATAWNY SOUP WITH MEATBALLS
### Serves 4

*1 onion, chopped*
*2 large carrots, sliced*
*1 cooking apple, peeled, cored and chopped*
*1 oz (25 g) butter*
*1½ tbsp plain flour*
*1 tsp curry paste*
*1 tbsp tomato puree*
*1¾ pt (1 litre) lamb stock*
*6 oz (175 g) lean minced lamb*
*1 egg, beaten*
*1 tsp garam masala*
*pinch cayenne pepper*
*1 tbsp chopped fresh oregano or 1 tsp dried*
*1 tbsp oil*
*fresh oregano leaves to garnish*

Sauté the onion, carrot and apple in the melted butter until soft. Stir in 1 tbsp flour, the curry paste and tomato puree, and cook gently, stirring, for about 2 minutes. Stir in the stock, bring to the boil, cover and simmer for 30 minutes. Season. While the soup is cooking, mix together the lamb, ½ tbsp flour, spices and enough of the beaten egg to make a firm mixture. Shape into 20 small balls with floured hands. Fry in hot oil for about 8 minutes until browned and cooked through. Drain on kitchen paper. Liquidise the soup and reheat with the meatballs added. Bring to the boil and simmer for 5 minutes.

# ARMENIAN SOUP
### Serves 4-6

*2 oz (50 g) red lentils, washed*
*2 oz (50 g) dried apricots, washed*
*1 large potato*
*2 pints (1.2 ltr) vegetable stock*
*juice of half a lemon*
*1 tsp ground cumin*
*3 tbsp chopped parsley*
*salt and pepper*

Place lentils and apricots in a large saucepan. Roughly chop the potato and add to the pan with the remaining ingredients. Bring to the boil, cover and simmer for 30 minutes. Allow to cool, then blend in a liquidiser until smooth. Reheat and serve, adjusting seasoning to taste.

# CORN AND CRAB SOUP
Serves 4

*1 oz (25 g) butter*
*1 onion, chopped*
*1½ pts (900 ml) chicken stock*
*12 oz (350 g) can sweetcorn, drained*
*salt and freshly ground black pepper*
*6 oz (175 g) can crab meat*

Melt the butter in a saucepan, add the onion and cook gently for 5 minutes, without colouring. Add the stock, sweetcorn, salt and pepper and bring to the boil, stirring. Cover the saucepan and simmer for 10 minutes or until the corn is tender. Liquidise the soup in a food processor or blender, then return to the saucepan and bring to the boil, stirring. Drain the crab meat, flake and remove any pieces of bone. Stir into the soup, bring to the boil, taste and check the seasoning. If the soup is too thick, stir in some extra stock. Serve very hot.

# FRENCH ONION SOUP
Serves 4-6

*2 oz (50 g) butter*
*4-5 medium onions, chopped*
*1-2 cloves garlic, crushed*
*¼ tsp sugar*
*1 oz (25 g) flour*
*2 pts (1.1 ltr) vegetable stock*
*¼ pt (150 ml) white wine (optional)*
*1 bay leaf*
*3-4 sprigs parsley*
*1 sprig thyme*
*a pinch of nutmeg*
*4-6 slices French bread*
*3-5 tbsp grated Gruyère, or Emmental mixed with Parmesan cheese*

Sauté the onions, garlic and a sprinkling of sugar in the melted butter and brown slowly, stirring to prevent burning. Stir in the flour and brown slightly. Add the stock, and wine, if using, stirring to a smooth consistency. Bring to the boil, add the herbs and seasoning and simmer for about 30 minutes. Remove the bay leaf and the sprigs of parsley and thyme. Cut the French bread into slices and put into the oven to dry and brown slightly, or grill gently. Pile the cheese on top of the slices and grill until it is just melting. Pour the soup into bowls and float a slice of bread on top of each bowl.

# BABY MARROW AND BACON SOUP
### Serves 4

*1 large onion, finely chopped*
*2 oz (50 g) butter*
*2 potatoes, diced*
*10 oz (300 g) baby marrows, diced*
*2 chicken or vegetable stock cubes*
*1³/₄ pt (1 litre) boiling water*
*4 fl oz (120 ml) cream*
*8 rashers back bacon, derinded*
*chopped chives or parsley*

Grill the rashers of bacon slowly until they are crisp. Sauté the onion in the butter until soft but not brown, then add the baby marrows and potatoes and toss in the butter. Dissolve the stock cubes in the boiling water and add to the vegetables. Cover the pan and bring to the boil. Reduce heat and simmer for about 30 minutes. Liquidise the vegetables and heat through again gently. Pour into warmed soup dishes and top with the crumbled crispy bacon and chopped herbs.

# WATERCRESS SOUP
### Serves 4

*2 bunches watercress*
*1 oz (25 g) butter*
*1 small onion, chopped*
*12 oz (350 g) potatoes, diced*
*¹/₂ oz (10 g) flour*
*³/₄ pt (450 ml) chicken stock*
*¹/₂ pt (300 ml) milk*
*salt and freshly ground pepper*
*pinch of powdered mace or small blade*
*5 oz (150 g) natural yoghurt or 5 fl oz (150 ml) single cream*

Wash and pick over the watercress, discarding any thick stems. Chop the leaves and remaining stalks. Reserve a few sprigs for garnish. Melt the butter and gently cook the potatoes and onion together for 3 minutes, then add the watercress and cook for a further 5 minutes, stirring occasionally to prevent browning. Sprinkle in the flour and blend well. Stir in the stock and milk together with the seasoning, bring to the boil and simmer gently for about 20 minutes or until the potato is tender. Puree in a blender or rub through a sieve, and reheat gently with 4 tbsp (60 ml) of yoghurt or cream. Pour into dishes and serve with a swirl of cream and watercress sprig on top.

# SPRING VEGETABLE SOUP
### Serves 4-6

*4 carrots, diced*
*2-3 leeks, well washed and sliced*
*8 spring onions, sliced*
*1½ oz (35 g) butter*
*¾ oz (15 g) flour*
*1½ pts (900 ml) vegetable or chicken stock*
*4 oz (110 g) cauliflower florets*
*2-3 tbsp peas*
*2-3 tbsp green beans, sliced*
*½ tsp sugar*
*2 tbsp mixed parsley, chervil, mint and thyme, chopped*
*¼ pt (150 ml) cream*
*2 egg yolks*

Sauté the carrots, leeks, and spring onions gently in melted butter without browning for 5 minutes. Sprinkle in the flour, blending in thoroughly and then add the stock, stirring well. Bring to the boil and simmer for a few minutes, then add the cauliflower florets, peas, beans and sugar. Simmer for 15 minutes. Add the herbs and cook for a few more minutes. Season to taste. Mix the cream thoroughly with the egg yolks. Mix a few tablespoons of the hot soup into the cream and egg yolks. Take the soup off the heat and strain the cream and egg yolk mixture back into the pan, stirring constantly. Reheat very gently to avoid curdling.

# MUSHROOM SOUP
### Serves 4

*1 oz (25 g) butter*
*1 oz (25 g) flour*
*½ pint (300 ml) chicken stock*
*½ pint (300 ml) milk*
*1 tbsp chopped fresh parsley*
*4 oz (110 g) mushrooms, wiped and finely chopped*
*salt and freshly ground pepper*
*1 tbsp lemon juice*
*2 tbsp fresh cream*

Place all ingredients except lemon juice and fresh cream in a large saucepan. Bring to the boil, whisking continuously, over moderate heat. Cover and simmer for 10 minutes. Remove from the heat and add the lemon juice and cream, stirring well. Serve with melba toast.

## CREAM OF CELERY SOUP
### Serves 4

*1 oz (25 g) butter*
*1 head celery, cleaned and finely chopped*
*celery leaves, reserved from above*
*2 onions, chopped*
*1 oz (25 g) flour*
*4 oz (110 g) low or medium fat cream cheese*
*1/2 pt (300 ml) chicken stock*
*1/2 pt (300 ml) milk*
*salt and white pepper*
*3 fl oz (90 ml) single cream*
*celery leaves to garnish*

Sauté the celery and onion gently for 5 minutes in the butter, shaking or stirring the pan frequently to prevent browning. Blend the cream cheese with a little of the stock until liquid and return to the pan together with the remaining stock, milk and seasoning. Bring to the boil and simmer for 30 minutes. Liquidise in a blender or rub through a sieve, return to the pan and gently reheat together with half the cream. Serve with a swirl of cream in each bowl, garnished with the reserved celery leaves.

## NETTLE SOUP
### Serves 4

*saucepanful of young nettles*
*1/4 pint (150 ml) water*
*1 small onion, peeled and chopped*
*2 oz (50 g) butter*
*2 oz (50 g) plain flour*
*1 pint (600 ml) chicken stock*
*salt and freshly ground pepper*
*1 tsp soured cream*

Wash the nettles carefully, but well, and press down into a large saucepan. Add the chopped onion and the water, cover and bring to the boil. Simmer gently for around 15 minutes, strain off the liquid and liquidise in a blender or food processor. Melt the butter in a saucepan and add the flour, cooking for 1 minute, stirring all the time. Add the chicken stock a little at a time, stir well and bring to the boil. Cook for a few minutes and then add the nettle puree and heat through. Just before serving stir in the soured cream and dust with a little chopped parsley if desired.

## POTATO AND CARAWAY SOUP
Serves 6

*2 large onions, finely chopped*
*4 oz (110 g) butter*
*1 lb (450 g) potatoes, peeled and diced*
*1 tbsp caraway seeds*
*2 bay leaves*
*1¼ pts (750 ml) chicken stock*
*2 oz (50 g) plain flour*
*1½ pts (900 ml) milk*
*½ pt (300 ml) single cream*
*salt and freshly ground black pepper*
*croutons & caraway seeds to garnish*

Sauté the onion in half the butter in a large pan until soft. Add the potatoes, caraway seeds and bay leaf and stir for a few minutes. Add the stock, cover, and simmer for 20 minutes. Melt the remaining butter in another pan, add the flour and cook, stirring, for 1 minute. Gradually add the milk, then bring to the boil and simmer for 5 minutes. Remove the bay leaves and liquidise half the potato mixture with half the white sauce. Pour into a clean pan and repeat with the rest of the two mixtures Stir in the cream, season well and reheat gently. Do not let it boil. Serve garnished with croutons and caraway seeds.

## CREAM OF SPINACH SOUP
Serves 6

*2 oz (50 g) butter*
*6 oz (175 g) packet frozen spinach (leaves or chopped)*
*1 onion, finely chopped*
*1 oz (25 g) flour*
*½ pint (300 ml) chicken stock*
*1 pt (600 ml) milk*
*salt and pepper*
*pinch of grated nutmeg*
*3 tbsp single cream*

Sauté the onions and spinach gently in melted butter for 5-6 minutes. Mix in the flour, stir thoroughly and remove from the heat. Add the stock, return to the heat and boil, stirring continuously, until the mixture thickens. Blend in the milk, and bring back to the boil. Cover and simmer for 15-20 minutes. Season. Liquidise the soup or put through a sieve, and thin with a little milk if required. Reheat gently and stir in fresh cream when ready to serve.

## SPLIT PEA AND HAM SOUP
### Serves 4

*2 pig's trotters, split (optional)*
*1 ham bone*
*8 oz (225 g) dried green split peas, soaked overnight in 1½ pts (900 ml) water*
*8 oz (225 g) potatoes, sliced*
*3 whole leeks, washed and sliced*
*3 celery sticks, sliced (reserve leaves)*
*salt and freshly ground pepper*
*2 tbsp chopped parsley*
*6 oz (175 g) cooked ham, diced*

Place the pig's trotters (if using) and the ham bone in a large saucepan. Cover with 1½ pts (900 ml) water and bring to the boil. Skim off any scum with a slotted spoon, then lower the heat and simmer for 1 hour. Add the peas and their soaking water. Continue to cook for about 20 minutes. Add the sliced potatoes, leeks (including the green parts) and celery and continue cooking for another 40 minutes until the peas are soft. Season to taste with salt and freshly ground pepper. Remove the ham bone and trotters from the pan. Scrape the meat from the bones, discarding fat and gristle. Return the meat to the pan. Thin the soup, if necessary, with a little extra liquid. Chop most of the reserved celery leaves and add to the soup with the chopped parsley and diced ham. Heat through, adjust seasoning and serve garnished with celery leaves.

## CREAM OF PARSLEY SOUP
### Serves 4

*1 oz (25 g) butter*
*4 oz (110 g) fresh parsley, roughly chopped*
*1 medium onion, thinly sliced*
*2 oz (50 g) celery, cleaned and sliced*
*4 level tsp flour*
*1¾ pints (1 litre) chicken stock*
*salt and freshly ground pepper*
*4 tbsp fresh single cream*

Sauté the onions, parsley and celery gently in melted butter. Cover and cook gently until the vegetables are quite soft, shaking the pan occasionally. Blend in the flour, then add the stock. Season and bring to the boil. Cover and simmer for about 25 minutes. Leave to cool slightly, then liquidise in a blender or rub through a sieve.

# CURRY SOUP
### Serves 6

*2 tbsp desiccated coconut*
*¼ pt (150 ml) boiling water*
*1 oz (25 g) butter*
*1 level tbsp curry powder*
*1 onion, finely chopped*
*1 oz (25 g) flour*
*1½ pts (900 ml) chicken stock*
*1½ lb (675 g) cooking apples, peeled, cored and roughly chopped*
*juice of half a lemon*
*1 tbsp redcurrant jelly*
*salt and pepper*
*chopped parsley*

Put the coconut in a bowl, pour on boiling water and infuse for 20 minutes. Meanwhile melt the butter in a saucepan, add the curry powder and onion, cover and cook gently, stirring occasionally, for 10 minutes. Stir in the flour and cook for a minute, then add the stock and bring to the boil, stirring until thickened. Strain the liquor from the coconut and add to the soup (discarding the coconut). Add the apples, lemon juice, redcurrant jelly and seasoning. Cover the pan and simmer for 15 minutes or until the apples are tender. Puree the soup in a food processor or blender in 2 or 3 batches. Rinse out the saucepan, return the soup to it and bring to the boil. Taste and check seasoning, adding a little extra stock if the soup is too thick. Pour into a tureen and sprinkle with parsley.

# TUNA CHOWDER
### Serves 4

*10½ oz (310 g) can condensed tomato soup*
*10½ oz (310 g) can condensed cream of chicken soup*
*1 pt (600 ml) water*
*8 oz (225 g) can peas, drained*
*2 tbsp dried onion flakes*
*7 oz (200 g) can tuna fish, drained and flaked*
*1 oz (25 g) quick cooking macaroni*
*salt and pepper*

Put all the ingredients in a saucepan and bring to the boil, stirring. Cover the saucepan and simmer for 10 minutes, or until the macaroni is cooked. Taste, check seasoning and serve at once.

## STILTON SOUP
Serves 6

*2 oz (50 g) butter*
*1 onion, finely chopped*
*2 celery sticks, finely chopped*
*1½ oz (35 g) plain flour*
*3 tbsp dry white wine*
*1½ pts (900 ml) chicken stock*
*½ pt (300 ml) milk*
*4 oz (110 g) Blue Stilton cheese, crumbled*
*2 oz (50 g) Cheddar cheese, grated*
*salt and pepper*
*4 tbsp double cream*
*croutons to garnish*

Sauté the vegetables in the melted butter until soft but not browned. Stir in the flour and cook for 1 minute. Add the wine and stock, stirring all the time to stop the soup from forming lumps. Bring to the boil, and simmer for 30 minutes. Add the milk and cheeses, stirring constantly. Season and stir in the cream. Puree in a blender or rub through a sieve, return to the pan and reheat gently. Serve garnished with croutons.

## WHITE BEAN SOUP WITH SMOKED SAUSAGE
Serves 4

*2 onions, chopped*
*1 tbsp cooking oil*
*1 tbsp plain flour*
*4 oz (110 g) small haricot beans, soaked overnight*
*1 pt (600 ml) chicken stock*
*14 oz (400 g) can tomatoes*
*8 oz (225 g) smoked sausage, cut into bite-size chunks*
*½ tsp dried thyme*
*salt and freshly ground black pepper*

Drain the beans. Sauté the onions gently in the oil until softened, but do not let them brown. Stir in the flour, blend well and then add the beans. Gradually stir in the stock, bring to the boil and simmer for 2-3 minutes. Add the canned tomatoes, chopped, together with the liquid in the can, the sausage, thyme and seasoning. Cover and simmer for 1½ hours or until the beans are tender. Serve with crusty bread and butter.

## PUMPKIN SOUP
### Serves 4

*2 oz (50 g) butter*
*1 large onion*
*1 lb (450 g) pumpkin*
*2 large, ripe tomatoes*
*1 tbsp sugar*
*2 pints (1.2 ltr) milk*
*salt and freshly ground black pepper*
*4 tbsp single cream*
*parsley to garnish, and croutons for serving*

Peel and deseed the pumpkin, then dice. Blanch, skin and seed the tomatoes, then chop the flesh. Chop onion. Melt half the butter in a heavy-based saucepan, stir in the vegetables and cook for 2-3 minutes. Sprinkle in the sugar and add a small glass of water. Cover and cook gently for about 30 minutes, or until the vegetables are soft. Meanwhile, bring the milk to the boil in a large saucepan, then keep hot. Add half the milk to the cooked vegetables and blend, pour the mixture into the pan with the remaining hot milk and whisk. Season to taste with salt and freshly ground black pepper, then stir in the cream. Keep the soup hot over a gentle heat. Just before serving, whisk in the remaining butter and sprinkle on the croutons and chopped parsley.

## CHESTNUT SOUP
### Serves 6

*2 oz (50 g) margarine*
*1 onion, chopped*
*1 lb (450 g) chestnuts, peeled and roughly chopped*
*2 oz (50 g) flour*
*2 pt (1.2 litres) vegetable or chicken stock*
*grated rind and juice of 1 lemon*
*few drops gravy browning or brown colouring*
*¼ pt (150 ml) plain fromage frais*

Soften the onions and chestnuts in the melted margarine for 5 minutes. Add the flour, stir well for 2 minutes and then gradually stir in the stock. Season. Bring to the boil, stirring, until the soup thickens. Cover and simmer for 30 minutes or until the chestnuts are soft. Liquidise in a blender or rub through a sieve, return to the pan and stir in the lemon rind and juice and gravy browning. Reheat gently, season to taste and then stir in the fromage frais.

## SPANISH FISH SOUP
### Serves 6-8

*2 tbsp oil*
*2 large onions, chopped*
*1 yellow pepper, skinned and chopped*
*2 cloves garlic, crushed*
*2 x 14 oz (400 g) cans tomatoes*
*2 tbsp lemon juice*
*2 tbsp Worcestershire sauce*
*1 pt (600 ml) tomato juice*
*½ pt (300 ml) water*
*1 bay leaf*
*salt and freshly ground black pepper*
*12 oz (350 g) white fish*
*chopped parsley to garnish*

Grill the pepper until the skin blisters and blackens, and skin when it's cool enough to handle, removing the seeds. Sauté the onion and garlic in the oil for about 5 minutes until soft. Add the chopped pepper flesh, tomatoes, lemon and tomato juice and the rest of the seasonings together with the water. Bring to the boil, cover the pan and simmer gently for about 10 minutes. Meanwhile, skin the fish, remove any bones and cut into small pieces. Add to the soup and cook very gently for another 10 minutes or until the fish is cooked. Remove the bay leaf and add seasoning to taste. Serve sprinkled with chopped parsley.

## TOMATO AND ONION SOUP
### Serves 4

*8 oz (225 g) onions, sliced*
*8 oz (225 g) tomatoes, skinned and chopped*
*1 pt (600 ml) chicken stock*
*salt and pepper*
*3 level tbsp dried skimmed milk*

Put the onions and tomatoes in a pan with the stock and seasoning, bring to the boil and simmer, covered, for about 30 minutes. Liquidise in a blender or rub through a sieve, whisk in the milk powder and reheat gently. Serve sprinkled with chopped parsley.

# CHICKEN AND TARRAGON SOUP
### Serves 4

*carcass and bones of a chicken*
*1 onion, peeled and pierced with 4 cloves*
*1 carrot, thinly sliced*
*2 cloves garlic, crushed*
*1 stick celery, cleaned and finely sliced*
*1 bouquet garni*
*12 fl oz (360 ml) dry white wine*
*8 peppercorns*
*1 bunch tarragon, including the stalks*
*1 chicken breast fillet*
*¼ pt (150 ml) carton single cream*
*1 egg*
*1 level tsp caster sugar*

Prepare this soup the day before serving. Put the chicken carcass in a large pan with the onion, carrot, garlic, celery, bouquet garni, white wine and peppercorns and the tarragon stalks. Bring to the boil, skim if necessary, and simmer for about 1½ hours, adding more water if necessary. Remove the carcass, strain the stock, leave to cool, then refrigerate. To make the soup, skim the fat off the top of the jellied stock, return to the saucepan and reduce to 1¼ pints. Cut the chicken breast into small pieces and simmer in the prepared stock for about 10 minutes, or until tender. Liquidise. Return to the pan adding the cream, egg yolk and a handful of chopped tarragon leaves and then liquidise again until the soup turns a pale green. Season and reheat very gently. Serve sprinkled with tarragon leaves and a swirl of cream.

# CARROT AND LEEK SOUP
### Serves 4

*2 carrots*
*2 large leeks*
*1 oz (25 g) butter*
*1 tsp horseradish sauce*
*1 oz (25 g) medium oatmeal*
*mace (or bay leaf)*
*1 pt (600 ml) stock*
*¼ pt (150 ml) milk*

Slice the carrots and leeks. Sauté in butter for about 7 minutes. Add horseradish sauce, oatmeal, salt, pepper and mace (or bay leaf). Pour on the stock and milk. Bring to the boil and simmer for 25 minutes.

# MINESTRONE
Serves 6

*3 oz (75 g) dried haricot beans, which have been soaked overnight*
*2-3 tbsp olive oil*
*1-2 cloves garlic, crushed*
*1 medium onion, sliced*
*2 slices bacon, diced*
*2 pts (1.2 ltr) vegetable stock*
*1 stalk celery, finely sliced*
*1 leek, white part only, cut into shreds*
*2-3 oz (50-75 g) cabbage, chopped*
*1-2 courgettes, cut in strips*
*1 can tomatoes (or 4 fresh tomatoes, skinned and chopped)*
*1 level tsp tomato puree*
*6 green beans, chopped*
*3 tbsp peas*
*2 oz (50 g) macaroni*
*2 level tbsp mixed parsley, marjoram, oregano and basil, chopped*
*grated Parmesan cheese to garnish.*

Bring the beans to the boil, covered, with 2 cups of slightly salted water. Simmer for 2 hours or until tender, adding a little more water if necessary. In another pan heat the oil and cook the onion, garlic and bacon until golden brown. Add to the bean pot, together with the stock, celery and leek. Cook for 20 minutes. Then add the finely sliced cabbage, courgettes, chopped tomatoes, tomato puree, green beans, peas, macaroni and chopped herbs. Cook for 20 minutes. Season to taste, and serve with plenty of grated Parmesan on the side.

# CREAM OF TURNIP SOUP
Serves 4-6

*8 oz (225 g) young turnips, sliced*
*2 medium potatoes, sliced*
*1 small onion, sliced*
*1½ oz (35 g) butter*
*¾ oz (15 g) flour*
*1¼ pts (750 ml) chicken stock*
*½ pt (300 ml) milk*
*1 level tbsp chopped parsley and 2 slices of bacon to garnish*

Soften the turnips, potatoes and onion in the melted butter for 20-30 minutes. Do not brown. Sprinkle in the flour, blend it in thoroughly, pour on the stock and stir well. Bring to the boil and simmer for 15 minutes. Liquidise in a blender or rub through a sieve. Reheat, season to taste and add the milk. Derind the bacon and cut into small pieces. Fry the bacon in a dry frying pan until it is crisp and golden. Serve the soup sprinkled with chopped parsley and crumbled bacon.

# BACON AND SPINACH SOUP
Serves 6

*2 oz (50 g) butter*
*1 large onion, chopped*
*6 oz (175 g) streaky bacon, chopped*
*1 lb (450 g) frozen spinach*
*1 oz (25 g) flour*
*¾ pt (450 ml) milk*
*¾ pt (450 ml) chicken stock*
*1 tbsp Worcestershire sauce*
*salt and freshly ground black pepper*
*¼ pt (150 ml) single cream*

Heat the butter in a large saucepan, add the onion and bacon and fry gently for about 5 minutes until soft. Add the spinach, cover the pan and cook gently for 10 minutes. Stir the flour into the spinach and cook for a minute. Gradually add the milk and stock, stirring constantly. Add the Worcestershire sauce and seasoning, bring to the boil, cover and simmer for 20 minutes. Puree the soup in a blender or food processor. Rinse out the saucepan, return the soup to it and bring to the boil. Taste and check seasoning. Remove the pan from the heat and stir in all but a tablespoon of the cream. Turn into a serving dish or tureen and swirl the remaining cream on top.

## SMOKED SALMON SOUP
### Serves 8

*2 oz (50 g) onion, chopped*
*2 oz (50 g) unsalted butter*
*1 bay leaf*
*5 level tbsp plain flour*
*4 pints (2.4 litres) fish stock*
*juice of half lemon*
*8 oz (225 g) low fat soft cheese with garlic & herbs*
*8 oz (225 g) smoked salmon pieces*
*3 oz (75 g) cooked, peeled prawns*
*salt and freshly ground pepper*
*crème fraîche, salmon roe and dill sprigs to garnish*

Melt the butter in a large saucepan and sauté the onion and bay leaf, stirring, for 7-8 minutes until softened but not browned. Stir in the flour, stock and lemon juice, bring to the boil, stirring, then turn the heat down and simmer for 4-5 minutes until thickened. Take off the heat and whisk in the soft cheese, smoked salmon pieces, prawns and ground pepper. Pour into a large bowl, cool, cover and leave in the refrigerator overnight. Liquidise the smoked salmon mixture in a blender or food processor and then push through a sieve to extract the flavoured liquid. Adjust the seasoning and return to a saucepan to reheat gently. Garnish with crème fraîche, salmon roe and dill sprigs.

## CARROT AND WATERCRESS SOUP
### Serves 4

*1 large onion, chopped*
*1 oz (25 g) butter*
*1½ lb (675 g) carrots, chopped*
*1 bunch watercress, washed, picked and roughly chopped*
*2 tbsp flour*
*2 pts (1.2 litres) vegetable stock*
*natural yoghurt and watercress leaves to garnish*

Sauté the onion in the butter for about 4 minutes, then add the chopped carrots and cook gently for another 4 minutes, stirring from time to time. Blend in the flour, add the vegetable stock, bring to the boil and simmer, covered, for about 25 minutes or until the carrots are soft. Liquidise in a blender or rub through a sieve and return to the pan. Add the chopped watercress, reserving a few leaves for garnish, and cook for a further 4 minutes. Serve garnished with a swirl of natural yoghurt, and a few watercress leaves.

# OXTAIL SOUP
Serves 4

*1 oxtail*
*1 carrot, chopped*
*1 stick celery, chopped*
*2 oz (50 g) butter*
*1 bouquet garni*
*6 peppercorns*
*2 cloves*
*8 oz (225 g) lean bacon*
*4 pints (2.4 ltr) stock*
*2 oz (50 g) flour*
*half lemon*
*salt and pepper*
*1/2 tsp cayenne pepper*

Wash the tail, put into cold water and bring to the boil. Drain, dry and divide into joints. Fry these with the vegetables. Place the oxtail and vegetable mixture in a large pan with the bouquet garni, spices, bacon and stock. Simmer for five hours. Strain, and when cold skim off all the fat. Return the stock to the pan and bring to the boil, adding the flour mixed to a smooth paste with a little water. Sieve or blend the vegetables and add to the stock. Boil for 4 minutes. Season with lemon juice, salt, black pepper and cayenne. Remove the meat from the oxtail bones and add to the soup with the vegetables.

# THICK LEEK BROTH
Serves 4-6

*1 1/2 pt (900 ml) stock*
*8 oz (225 g) potatoes, peeled and diced*
*4 oz (110 g) carrots, diced*
*4 oz (110 g) swede or parsnips, diced*
*2 leeks, sliced*
*2 tbsp oatmeal*
*half small cabbage, shredded*
*salt and pepper*
*chopped parsley to garnish*

Boil the potatoes, carrots and swede or parsnips in the stock and cook for about 10 minutes. Add the leeks and cabbage. Mix the oatmeal with a little cold water and add. Bring back to the boil and simmer for 20 minutes until the vegetables are cooked. Adjust seasoning if required. Serve sprinkled with the chopped parsley.

## LENTIL SOUP
### Serves 6

*1 large onion, chopped*
*3 carrots, chopped*
*3 sticks celery, chopped*
*1 tbsp olive oil*
*14 oz (400 g) tin tomatoes, chopped*
*12 oz (350 g) lentils*
*1 clove garlic, crushed*
*1 tbsp chopped parsley*
*1/2 tsp ground cumin*
*1 bay leaf*
*3 pts water*
*2 vegetable stock cubes*

Sauté the onion, carrot and celery in the oil for 5 minutes. Add all the other ingredients and bring to the boil. Simmer very gently for 30-40 minutes until the lentils are cooked. Stir the soup frequently, as lentils tend to burn easily. Serve with granary bread or rolls.

## GERMAN POTATO SOUP
### Serves 4

*4 streaky bacon rashers, chopped*
*1 onion, thinly sliced*
*8 oz (225 g) potatoes, diced*
*1 pt (600 ml) beef stock*
*1 bay leaf*
*salt and freshly ground black pepper*
*good pinch mace or grated nutmeg*
*3-4 frankfurters, sliced*
*1 tbsp chopped parsley*

Fry the bacon gently in a saucepan until the fat begins to run. Add the onion and continue cooking until it has softened. Stir in the potatoes, stock, bay leaf, and seasonings. Bring to the boil, cover and simmer gently for about 25 minutes or until the potato is cooked. Add the frankfurters, taste and adjust seasoning and simmer for a further 5 minutes. Remove the bay leaf. Stir in most of the parsley and serve sprinkled with the remainder.

## BARLEY CREAM SOUP
Serves 4

2 oz (50 g) pearl barley
1 small carrot, chopped
1 small onion, chopped
1 stick celery, chopped
1 oz (25 g) butter
2 pts (1.2 litres) chicken stock
1 egg
1/4 pt (150 ml) milk
salt and pepper

Wash the barley, add to the stock and bring to the boil. Melt the butter and cook the vegetables over a low heat for a few minutes, keeping the lid on the pan and shaking occasionally. Add the barley and stock and simmer for 2 hours. Blend or rub through a sieve if a smoother texture is desired. Add the egg and milk beaten together and reheat very gently without boiling. Season and serve sprinkled with chopped parsley.

## CREAM OF PARSNIP SOUP
Serves 6

3 oz (75 g) butter
1 onion, chopped
1 lb (450 g) parsnip, cubed
1 oz (25 g) flour
1 rounded tsp curry powder
2 pts (1.2 ltr) beef stock
salt and pepper
1/4 pt (150 ml) single cream
chopped parsley

Melt the butter in a large saucepan, add the onion and parsnip and fry gently for 10 minutes. Stir in the flour and curry powder and cook for a minute, then add the stock and seasoning and bring to the boil, stirring. Cover the saucepan and simmer gently for 25 minutes or until the parsnip is tender. Puree the soup in a blender in 2 or 3 batches. Rinse out the saucepan and return the soup to it. Reheat, taste and check seasoning. When ready to serve, remove from the heat and stir in the cream. Pour into a tureen and sprinkle with chopped parsley.

## TUSCAN CABBAGE SOUP
Serves 4-6

*1 large onion, chopped*
*2 medium carrots, chopped*
*2 sticks celery, chopped*
*1 small bulb fennel, chopped*
*1 tbsp olive oil*
*1 clove garlic, crushed*
*1 tsp dried thyme*
*1/2 tsp dried rosemary*
*2 pts (1.2 ltr) hot stock*
*14 oz (400 g) can tomatoes*
*1 tbsp tomato puree*
*salt and freshly ground black pepper*
*4 oz (110 g) dark green cabbage, shredded*
*Parmesan cheese to garnish*

Sauté the onion, carrot, celery and fennel slowly in the oil for about 10 minutes, adding the garlic, thyme and rosemary about half-way through. Pour in the hot stock, add the tomatoes, and the puree, cover and simmer for 30 minutes. Season well. Add the cabbage to the soup and cook gently for 5 minutes. Serve sprinkled with Parmesan cheese. To make into a main meal: add 8 oz (225 g) sliced courgettes and 2 sliced leeks with an extra 1 pt (600 ml) stock. Stir in a 15 oz (425 g) can of rinsed and drained cannellini or haricot beans with the cabbage. Serve with a thick slice of wholemeal bread in each soup bowl.

## ORANGE VEGETABLE SOUP
Serves 4-6

*1 lb (450 g) pumpkin, marrow and carrots mixed*
*8 oz (225 g) celeriac*
*3 pts (2 litres) chicken stock*
*1 oz (25 g) butter*

Peel the vegetables and cut into pieces. Process in a food processor until finely chopped. Tip into a saucepan, add chicken stock and seasoning and bring to the boil. Cover and simmer for 20 minutes or until the vegetables are tender. Return to the food processor and liquidise or rub through a sieve until smooth. Reheat in the saucepan, stirring in the butter in small pieces just before serving.

# CHICK PEA SOUP
## Serves 4-6

*1 lb (450 g) dried chick peas, soaked overnight, rinsed and drained*
*3½ pints (2 ltr) water*
*6 tbsp olive oil*
*2 large onions, peeled and sliced*
*2 carrots, washed and thinly sliced*
*2 cloves garlic, peeled and thinly sliced*
*2 tbsp tomato puree*
*2 large tomatoes, skinned and sliced*
*2 sticks celery, chopped*
*salt and freshly ground black pepper*
*2 tbsp lemon juice*

Put the chick peas in a large saucepan, cover with water and bring to the boil. Cover and boil rapidly for 15 minutes. Drain and discard the liquid. Return the chick peas to the pan, add 3½ pints (2 litres) of water and bring to the boil again. Skim any scum off the surface, cover and simmer for about 1¾ hours or until the chickpeas are tender. Meanwhile, heat the oil in a saucepan and sauté the onions, carrots and garlic over low heat for about 6 minutes, stirring frequently, until they are soft but not brown. Stir in the tomato puree and sliced tomatoes and cook for 5 minutes. Remove about 4 tbsp of the chick peas with a slotted spoon and reserve. Stir the vegetable mixture into the chick peas. Liquidise the soup in a food processor or blender, return to the pan and add the reserved chick peas. Reheat gently, stirring in the lemon juice and salt and pepper to taste.

# MUSHROOM AND WATERCRESS SOUP
## Serves 4

*2 oz (50 g) butter*
*1½ oz (35 g) flour*
*8 oz (225 g) mushrooms, finely chopped*
*2 tbsp chopped watercress*
*1 pint (600 ml) chicken stock*
*¾ pint (450 ml) milk*
*salt and freshly ground pepper*

Melt the butter in a saucepan, add the flour and cook gently for 3-4 minutes. Blend in the chicken stock and heat, stirring continuously, until the soup thickens and boils. Add the milk, mushrooms and watercress. Cook for a further 5 minutes, then season to taste.

# CUCUMBER SOUP WITH TROUT QUENELLES
Serves 4

*1 large onion*
*1 lb (450 g) cucumber, chopped*
*2 oz (50 g) chopped dill pickle*
*1 tbsp flour*
*1 pt (600 ml) milk*
*1/2 tsp dried dill*
*1 vegetable stock cube, crumbled*

*Quenelles:*
*8 oz (225 g) smoked trout fillets*
*4 oz (110 g) Cheddar cheese, grated*
*4 egg whites*
*salt and pepper*

Sauté the onion in butter until soft and blend in the flour, stirring well. Stir in the milk, then add the cucumber, dill pickle, dried dill and stock cube. Season. Simmer gently for 10 minutes, and then puree in a blender or rub through a sieve until smooth. Put to one side. To make the quenelles, mash the trout fillets and cheese together in a bowl or liquidise in a blender, and add plenty of seasoning. Whisk the egg whites lightly and fold into the mixed trout and cheese. Bring a pan of water to simmering point, drop in about 24 teaspoonfuls of the mixture, 8 at a time, and cook for 2 minutes. Lift out with a slotted spoon, drain and sprinkle with a little extra cheese. Grill until golden. Gently reheat the soup and serve with about 6 quenelles in each bowl.

# CREAM OF ONION SOUP
Serves 4

*1 oz (25 g) butter*
*1 lb (450 g) onions, thinly sliced*
*1 pt (600 ml) milk*
*salt and pepper*
*4 level tsp cornflour*
*3 tbsp single cream*
*1/4 tsp mace*

Sauté the onions gently in melted butter until soft but not browned - about 10 minutes. Blend in the cornflour and add the milk, 1/2 pt (300 ml) water and seasoning, stirring all the time to prevent lumps forming. Bring to the boil and simmer for 15-20 minutes, stirring from time to time. Add the cream, check seasoning and serve.

# KIDNEY SOUP
Serves 4

*1 onion, chopped*
*2 tbsp oil*
*1 large leek, sliced*
*1 large carrot, chopped*
*1 turnip or small swede, chopped*
*8 oz (225 g) ox kidney, chopped with core removed*
*1 tsp German mustard*
*1 bay leaf*
*salt and freshly ground black pepper*
*1³/₄ pts (1 litre) beef stock*
*croutons and chopped parsley to garnish*

Sauté the onion in the oil for a few minutes, then add the vegetables
and cook gently for a further 4 minutes. Add the kidney, mustard,
bay leaf and seasoning and stir well to brown the kidney slightly.
Gradually add the stock, bring to the boil, cover and simmer for
1 hour. Remove the bay leaf and liquidise the soup in a blender or rub
through a sieve. Return to the pan and reheat gently. Serve sprinkled
with crisply fried croutons and chopped parsley.

# FAST CELERY AND PRAWN BISQUE
Serves 6

*2 oz (50 g) butter*
*1 onion, sliced*
*8 oz (225 g) potatoes, diced*
*1 lb 2 oz (500 g) can celery hearts*
*1¹/₄ pt (750 ml) milk*
*1 level tsp paprika*
*salt and pepper*
*4 oz (110 g) frozen prawns, thawed*

Melt the butter in a saucepan, add the onion and potato and cook
gently for 5 minutes, so that they soften but do not brown. Stir in the
contents of the can of celery with the milk, paprika and seasoning and
bring to the boil. Stir with a wooden spoon to break down the celery
slightly. Reduce the heat, cover the pan and simmer for 25 minutes.
Liquidise the soup in a blender or food processor, and then rinse out
the saucepan and return the soup to it. Bring to the boil and stir in the
prawns. Simmer for a few minutes until the prawns are cooked
through. Taste and check seasoning. Turn into a tureen and serve very
hot.

# SPINACH AND POTATO SOUP WITH GARLIC
### Serves 4

*2 leeks, washed and sliced*
*1 lb (450 g) potatoes, cubed*
*2 oz (50 g) butter*
*3 cloves garlic, crushed*
*8 oz (225 g) spinach, washed and trimmed*
*1 pt (600 ml) vegetable stock*
*salt and freshly ground black pepper*
*10 fl oz (300 ml) milk*
*3 tbsp parsley, chopped*

Soften the leeks and potatoes in the melted butter without browning for about 5 minutes. Add the garlic, stir and cook for a minute. Then add the spinach a handful at a time. When the spinach has wilted down, pour in the stock, season and bring to the boil. Cover the pan and simmer for 20 minutes until the potatoes are soft. Liquidise the soup or rub through a sieve, and return to the pan, adding the milk and parsley. Reheat gently.

# BELGIAN VEGETABLE SOUP
### Serves 4-6

*2 medium potatoes, diced*
*1 onion, sliced*
*2 leeks, sliced*
*2 medium carrots, sliced*
*2 pts (1.2 litres) stock*
*half a cauliflower, cut into florets*
*4 oz (110 g) frozen green beans*
*4 oz (110 g) frozen peas*
*2 tsp dried thyme*
*salt and ground black pepper*

Place the potatoes, onion, leeks and carrots in a large pan with the stock, bring to the boil and simmer for 15 minutes. Add the cauliflower, beans, peas, thyme and seasoning, and simmer for another 15 minutes. To make into a main meal: mix together 12 oz (350 g) lean minced beef and 1 tsp each of ground nutmeg and cinnamon. Shape into about 32 tiny balls. Bring a large shallow pan of water or stock to the boil and poach the meatballs in batches in the simmering water. They take 2-3 minutes. Remove with a draining spoon and add to the vegetable soup just before serving. Hand round grated Gouda cheese for sprinkling on top.

## CURRIED POTATO AND APPLE SOUP
Serves 4

2 oz (50 g) butter or margarine
4 medium potatoes, peeled and diced
2 eating apples, peeled, cored and diced
2 tsp curry powder
2 pints (1.2 ltr) vegetable stock
salt and pepper
¼ pint (150 ml) natural yoghurt

Melt the butter or margarine in a large pan. Add the potatoes and
apples and fry gently for about 10 minutes until lightly browned. Add
the curry powder and fry gently for 1-2 minutes. Pour in the stock
and bring to the boil. Add salt and pepper to taste. Cover the pan and
simmer for about 25 minutes until the potatoes and apples are really
soft. Sieve or liquidise the soup then return it to the pan. Stir half the
yoghurt (at room temperature) into the soup, warm through and
adjust seasoning. Swirl in the remaining yoghurt when ready to serve.

## CREAM OF ARTICHOKE SOUP
Serves 4-6

2 lb (900 g) Jerusalem artichokes
2 slices of lemon
1 oz (25 g) butter
1 medium onion, chopped
2 level tbsp cornflour
¾ pt (450 ml) milk
2 tbsp lemon juice
2 tbsp fresh parsley, chopped
4 tbsp single cream

Wash and peel the artichokes and place in a large saucepan with
1½ pts (900 ml) cold salted water and the lemon slices. Bring to the
boil and simmer gently for 25 minutes until tender. Drain, reserve the
cooking liquid and make this up to 1 pt (600 ml) with water, discarding the lemon slices. Mash the artichokes. Sauté the onion in the butter until soft but not brown. Stir in the cornflour and gradually add
the reserved cooking water and milk. Add the artichokes and bring to
the boil, stirring. Cook for 2-3 minutes, then leave to cool. Puree in a
blender or rub through a sieve and return to a clean pan. Stir in the
lemon juice, cream and chopped parsley. Season to taste. Reheat gently, taking care not to let it boil. Garnish with croutons.

## KIDNEY BEAN SOUP
### Serves 4-6

*8 oz (225 g) kidney beans, soaked overnight*
*2 oz (50 g) butter*
*1 carrot, chopped*
*1 onion, chopped*
*4 tomatoes, skinned and chopped*
*1 tbsp tomato puree*
*pinch of mixed herbs*
*3 pts (1.8 litres) vegetable stock*
*grated cheese, to garnish*

Sauté the onions for a few minutes, then add the chopped carrot, beans and seasonings and cook, turning over in the butter, for about 5 minutes. Then add the chopped tomatoes, tomato puree and herbs. Stir well, pour in the vegetable stock and simmer for 2 -3 hours or until the beans are soft. Liquidise in a blender or rub through a sieve, season and serve sprinkled with grated cheese.

## CHINESE HOT AND SOUR SOUP
### Serves 4

*2 pts (1.2 litres) chicken stock*
*2 oz (50 g) canned sliced bamboo shoots, drained and chopped*
*1 carrot, cut into strips*
*2 large flat mushrooms, cut into thin strips*
*1 tsp dry sherry*
*2 tbsp red wine vinegar*
*2 tsp light soy sauce*
*1 tsp finely chopped fresh ginger*
*freshly ground black pepper*
*2 tbsp cornflour*
*4 tsp water*
*1 egg, beaten*
*2 spring onions, sliced*

Bring the stock to the boil in a large pan. Add the bamboo shoots, carrots and mushrooms, cover and simmer for 10 minutes. Add the sherry, vinegar, soy sauce, ginger and seasoning and bring back to the boil. Blend the cornflour with the water, stir into the soup and simmer for a few minutes until the soup thickens. Pour the beaten egg through a small sieve so that it trickles into the soup to make egg threads. Ladle the soup into bowls and sprinkle with spring onions.

## CREME DE FROMAGE
Serves 4

*1 tbsp finely chopped onion*
*2 oz (50 g) butter*
*2 tbsp plain flour*
*¾ pint (450 ml) chicken stock*
*8 oz (225 g) cooked carrots, pureed*
*¾ pint (450 ml) milk*
*4 oz (110 g) grated cheese*
*salt and freshly ground pepper*
*chopped parsley to garnish*

Sauté the onion in the butter until softened but not coloured. Stir in the flour and cook for about 1 minute. Gradually blend in the stock and the carrot puree. Continue cooking gently, stirring from time to time and add the milk. Add the cheese and stir over very low heat until it has melted. Season well and garnish with chopped parsley.

## SHRIMP SOUP
Serves 4-6

*1½ oz (35 g) butter*
*1½ oz (35 g) flour*
*1½ pts (900 ml) milk*
*2 tsp anchovy essence*
*salt*
*freshly ground black pepper*
*2 x 1.76 oz (50 g) cartons potted shrimps*
*2 tsp tomato puree*
*1 tbsp chopped parsley*

Melt the butter in a saucepan, stir in the flour and cook for one minute. Add the milk and anchovy essence and bring to the boil, stirring. Season and add the potted shrimps with the tomato puree, stirring well so that the puree colours the soup a delicate pink. Simmer gently for 5 minutes, stirring occasionally, so that the butter from the shrimps melts and flavours the soup. Taste and check seasoning, then pour into a tureen and serve very hot, sprinkled with chopped parsley.

## WHITE FISH SOUP
### Serves 4-6

*1 lb (450 g) white fish*
*2 pts (1.2 litres) fish stock*
*4 oz (110 g) each of onion, carrot and turnip, chopped*
*1 stick celery, chopped*
*1 bouquet garni*
*1 oz (25 g) flour*
*1/2 pt (300 ml) milk*
*1 tsp parsley, chopped*
*salt and black pepper*

Simmer the fish with the vegetables in the stock until both are cooked - about 1/2 hour. Strain. Return the stock to the pan and thicken with the flour mixed with the cold milk, stirring all the time. Bring to the boil and simmer for 5 minutes. Add seasoning and the flaked flesh of the fish. Serve sprinkled with the chopped parsley.

## TOMATO AND ORANGE SOUP
### Serves 6

*2 lb (900 g) tomatoes, fresh or canned*
*1 medium carrot, chopped*
*1 medium onion, chopped*
*1 medium orange*
*1 bay leaf*
*1 1/2 oz (35 g) butter*
*2 oz (50 g) flour*
*2 1/2 pts (1.5 litres) chicken stock*
*sugar to taste*
*1/4 pt (150 ml) cream*
*orange rind for garnish*

If using fresh tomatoes, grill or place in boiling water to remove skins. Remove seeds and chop the flesh. Sauté the onions and carrots for a few minutes in the melted butter, add the flour and blend well. Stir in the tomatoes, bay leaf and stock, cover the pan and simmer for about 1 hour. Add the strained juice of the orange. Reserve one quarter of the orange skin and grate the zest of the remaining skin. Add the zest to the soup. Liquidise in a blender or rub through a sieve and return to the pan with sugar to taste. Simmer for a further 5 minutes. Meanwhile, cut the reserved orange skin into very fine strips and blanch in boiling water for 6 minutes. Swirl the cream into the bowls of soup and sprinkle with the julienne of orange.

## WHITE BEAN SOUP
Serves 4

*6 oz (175 g) haricot beans*
*1 medium onion, finely chopped*
*1 clove garlic, crushed*
*2¹/₂ pints (1.4 ltr) chicken stock*
*¹/₂ tsp dried rosemary*
*4 oz (110 g) Red Leicester cheese, grated*
*salt and pepper*

Place the beans in a bowl and cover with boiling water. Leave for
3 hours. Drain. Place the onion in a large pan with the garlic, beans
and stock. Add the rosemary. Bring to the boil, cover and simmer
gently for 1-1¹/₂ hours or until the beans are tender. Puree half of the
stock and beans in a blender. Return the pureed soup to the pan, add
the cheese and adjust the seasoning.

## SCANDINAVIAN YELLOW PEA SOUP
Serves 4-6

*1 tbsp oil*
*6 rashers smoked bacon, derinded and chopped*
*2 stalks celery, chopped*
*2 medium carrots, chopped*
*2 potatoes, diced*
*2 onions, sliced*
*6 oz (175 g) yellow split peas, soaked overnight*
*2¹/₂ pts (1.4 litres) stock*
*1 tsp ground ginger*
*2 tsp whole grain mustard*
*freshly chopped parsley to garnish*

Heat the oil in a large pan and sauté the bacon until brown. Add the
vegetables and sauté for a further 5 minutes. Add the soaked peas to
the pan, pour in the stock and add the ginger and mustard. Bring to
the boil and simmer for about 45 minutes until the peas are soft. Sieve
or liquidise in a blender or food processor. Reheat, season to taste and
sprinkle with parsley. To make into a main meal: add about
8oz (225g) peeled and diced celeriac to the other vegetables. About
half way through the cooking time, add 8 oz (225 g) roughly chopped
lean gammon or bacon steaks and 5 minutes before the end of cooking, 4 oz (110 g) chopped frankfurters. Remove meat before liquidis-
ing then return to the soup afterwards. Add more stock or water if
necessary.

# CREAM OF VEGETABLE SOUP
### Serves 4

*2 oz (50 g) butter*
*8 oz (225 g) carrots, peeled and finely diced or grated*
*6 oz (175 g) swede, peeled and finely diced*
*2 small leeks, cleaned and finely chopped*
*1 oz (25 g) flour*
*³/₄ pt (450 ml) milk*
*6 tbsp single cream*
*chopped fresh parsley to garnish*

Melt the butter in a large pan and fry the carrots, swede and leeks for 5-10 minutes. Stir in the flour. Add the stock, salt and pepper and simmer for another 15-20 minutes, before adding the milk and fresh cream. Adjust seasoning and heat gently. Do not boil. Pour into warmed bowls and sprinkle with parsley. Serve with warm crusty bread or rolls.

# SPICED PUMPKIN SOUP
### Serves 4

*2 tbsp olive oil*
*1 large onion, chopped*
*2 lb (900g) pumpkin*
*2 tsp ground cumin*
*2 tsp ground coriander*
*2 in (5 cm) cinnamon stick*
*1 pint (600 ml) water*
*¹/₂ in (1 cm) piece fresh root ginger*
*Tabasco sauce*
*salt and freshly ground pepper*
*natural yoghurt and fresh coriander or parsley to garnish*

Sauté the onion in the olive oil until transparent. Peel and deseed the pumpkin, and cut into rough 1 in (2.5 cm) cubes. Dry fry the cumin and coriander in a heavy-based pan until an aroma is released. Add to the onion with the cinnamon stick and fry for one minute. Add the pumpkin, water and grated ginger, bring to the boil, reduce heat, cover and simmer for 30 minutes until the pumpkin is tender. Remove the cinnamon stick and blend until smooth. Reheat, adding water if necessary to obtain the desired consistency. Season to taste with a few dashes of Tabasco sauce, salt and freshly ground black pepper. Serve with a swirl of yoghurt and sprigs of fresh chopped parsley or coriander.

# GREEN PEA AND BACON CHOWDER
Serves 4

*1 medium onion, finely chopped*
*8 oz (225 g) streaky bacon, diced*
*1 oz (25 g) butter*
*8 oz (225 g) potatoes, diced*
*2 level tbsp flour*
*1 pt (600 ml) chicken stock*
*1 pt (600 ml) milk*
*salt and freshly ground pepper*
*8 oz (225 g) fresh peas*
*2 oz (50 g) freshly grated Parmesan cheese*
*snipped chives*

Sauté the onion and bacon in the melted butter until the onion is just golden, stir in the potato and cook for a further 4 minutes, shaking the pan from time to time. Add the flour, stirring, cook for 1 minute and then gradually add the stock and milk stirring all the time. Season and bring to the boil. Cover the pan and simmer gently for a further 15 minutes or until the potato is tender. Add the peas and continue simmering for another 15 minutes until they are cooked. Serve sprinkled with snipped chives, and a bowl of grated Parmesan cheese.

# KIDNEY AND BACON SOUP
Serves 6

*2 pig's kidneys*
*8 oz (225 g) streaky bacon*
*3 mushrooms, plus stalks*
*1 leek*
*2 pts (1.2 ltr) water*
*salt and freshly ground black pepper*
*1 tbsp flour*
*1 tbsp gravy powder or meat extract*
*chopped parsley and croutons to garnish*

Remove the gristle from the kidneys and chop very finely. Chop the bacon, leek, and mushrooms. Sauté the bacon gently until the fat runs, then add the other ingredients and continue cooking for another 3 minutes, stirring. Add water and seasoning and simmer for 35 minutes. Mix the flour and gravy powder or meat extract with a little cold water, blend with a tablespoon of the hot liquid and return to the pan. Bring to the boil and simmer for another 2 minutes. Check seasoning and sprinkle with chopped parsley. Serve with fried croutons.

## SPICED LENTIL SOUP
Serves 4-6

*1 medium onion*
*1 red pepper*
*2 sticks celery*
*8 oz (225 g) marrow or courgettes*
*4 oz (110 g) red lentils*
*1 tbsp oil*
*1 tsp paprika*
*1 tsp turmeric*
*pinch of cinnamon*
*pinch of cayenne pepper*
*14 oz (400 g) can of tomatoes*
*1 tsp basil*
*1 bay leaf*
*1¼ pts (750 ml) vegetable stock*
*salt and pepper*

Wash the lentils and pick them over for stones. Chop the vegetables.
Fry all the spices in heated oil then add the vegetables and lentils. Stir
and cook for about 5 minutes. Add the basil, bay leaf and tomatoes to
the vegetables with enough water or stock to make 2 pints (600 ml).
Bring to the boil and simmer for 40 minutes or until the lentils are
cooked. Adjust seasoning and add more stock or water if required.

## ONION AND AVOCADO SOUP
Serves 4-6

*2 oz (50 g) butter*
*1 large onion, chopped*
*1 clove garlic, crushed*
*1½ pts (900 ml) chicken stock*
*2 avocados*
*2 tbsp lemon juice*
*salt and pepper*
*¼ pt (150 ml) single cream*
*chopped parsley to garnish*

Cook the onion and garlic gently in the melted butter until soft but
not brown. Gradually stir in the stock and seasoning, bring to the boil
and simmer for 15 minutes. Peel the avocados and liquidise the flesh
in a blender or mash well together with the lemon juice. Stir into the
soup and simmer again for 5 minutes. Stir in the cream, making sure
that the soup does not boil. Garnish with chopped parsley.

## WINTER VEGETABLE WARMER
Serves 4

*1 small cabbage*
*1 lb (450g) carrots, peeled*
*8 oz (225 g) turnips, peeled*
*8 oz (225 g) swede, peeled*
*2 onions or leeks*
*2-3 celery sticks*
*1 rasher of bacon*
*3 oz (75 g) butter*
*4 oz (110 g) haricot beans, soaked overnight and drained*
*bouquet garni*
*vegetable stock or water*
*salt and pepper*
*chopped parsley and grated cheese to serve*

In a large pan dry-fry the bacon lightly. Add butter and heat until melted then add all the vegetables and fry for about 10 minutes, stirring. Add the bouquet garni, beans and stock to cover. Season well with pepper and bring to the boil. Cover and simmer for about 1 hour. Add the cabbage and salt to taste and cook for about 20 minutes adding more liquid if required. When all the ingredients are soft, remove the bouquet garni and adjust seasoning to taste. Garnish with the chopped parsley and grated cheese.

## BACON AND VEGETABLE SOUP
Serves 4-6

*1 lb (450 g) carrots, turnips, potato and parsnip, diced*
*1 oz (25 g) butter and a little oil*
*2 pts (1 ltr) ham or bacon stock*
*1 bay leaf*
*pinch of mixed dried herbs*
*freshly ground black pepper*
*4 oz (110 g) cooked ham or bacon, diced*
*1/4 pt (150 ml) single cream*
*salt to taste*

Melt the butter with the oil in a large saucepan and add the diced vegetables. Sauté until sealed and then sprinkle in a little flour. Stir until coated. Add the stock, bay leaf, herbs and pepper and bring to the boil. Cover the pan and simmer for about 25 minutes until the vegetables are tender. Add the diced ham or bacon. Taste and add salt if needed. Remove the bay leaf. Stir in the cream and reheat gently.

# CREAM OF CAULIFLOWER SOUP WITH CHEESE
### Serves 4

*1 cauliflower*
*1½ oz (35 g) butter or margarine*
*3 tbsp plain flour*
*1½ pt (900 ml) chicken stock*
*4 oz (110 g) Cheddar or Stilton cheese*
*salt and pepper*
*¼ pt (150 ml) single cream*
*pinch of grated nutmeg*

Divide the cauliflower into florets and wash thoroughly. Sauté the florets in the butter for a few minutes and set aside. Stir the flour into the butter and cook gently for 1-2 minutes. Remove from the heat and gradually blend in the stock. Bring to the boil, stirring and then simmer for about 3 minutes until thick and smooth. Return the cauliflower to the pan, season to taste, cover and simmer for about 30 minutes. Sieve or liquidise the soup, return to the pan and stir in the grated cheese, reserving a little for garnish. Add the single cream and nutmeg and reheat gently.

# EASY MUSHROOM SOUP
### Serves 4

*1 onion, chopped*
*12 oz (350 g) mushrooms, wiped and sliced*
*1 potato. peeled and chopped*
*2 tbsp oil*
*½ pt (300 ml) milk*
*¾ pt (450 ml) vegetable stock*
*½ tsp ground nutmeg*
*salt and freshly ground black pepper*
*chopped parsley to garnish*

Sauté the onion, mushrooms and potato gently in the oil for 5 minutes. Stir in the liquids and the seasonings. Bring to the boil, cover and cook gently for 10 minutes. When the vegetables are soft, liquidise or sieve to make a creamy soup. Serve sprinkled with chopped parsley and with crusty French bread.

## SMOKED SAUSAGE AND BEAN SOUP
### Serves 4

*1 large onion, finely chopped*
*1 clove garlic, crushed*
*1 tbsp oil*
*1¼ pts (750 litres) chicken stock*
*15 oz (425 g) can red kidney beans, drained*
*4 sticks celery, chopped*
*8 oz (225 g) smoked garlic sausage, chopped*
*1 level tsp thyme*
*salt and freshly ground black pepper*
*2 level tbsp cornflour*
*a little water*

Sauté the onion in the oil until softened. Add the sausage, kidney beans and celery and turn over in the oil for a few minutes. Sprinkle in the flour and blend well. Add the thyme and seasoning. Pour in the stock, stirring, bring to the boil, cover the pan, and simmer for 20 minutes. Serve with crisply fried croutons or crusty French bread.

## TOMATO AND BACON SOUP
### Serves 4

*1 oz (25 g) butter*
*1 medium onion, finely chopped*
*1 tsp sugar*
*3 rashers bacon, diced*
*1 tbsp tomato puree*
*3 tbsp fresh basil*
*1¼ pts (750 ml) chicken stock*
*2 x 14 oz (400 g) tins tomatoes*
*salt and freshly ground black pepper*
*Worcestershire sauce*
*double cream*
*chopped parsley and croutons to serve*

Sauté the onion together with the sugar (to caramelise the onion) and cook gently for 2 minutes. Add the bacon, tomato puree and basil. Add the tomatoes and stock and stir well. Cover the saucepan and leave to cook over a gentle heat for 30 minutes. Pass through a sieve or liquidise. Return to the pan, and add the Worcestershire sauce. Add cream to taste. Do not boil. Garnish with chopped parsley and croutons. Serve with hot garlic bread.

# SPICED LENTIL AND CARROT SOUP
### Serves 4

*2 oz (50 g) margarine*
*7 oz (200 g) carrots, grated*
*1 medium onion, finely sliced*
*10 whole green cardamoms*
*4 oz (110 g) lentils*
*2 pts (1.2 litres) chicken stock*
*salt and freshly ground pepper*

Melt the butter, add the carrots and onion and cook gently for 4-5 minutes. Meanwhile, split the cardamoms and remove their black seeds. Crush the seeds using a pestle and mortar, or use the end of a rolling pin on a wooden board. Add the crushed cardamom seeds and the lentils to the vegetables. Cook, stirring, for a further 1-2 minutes. Add the chicken stock and bring to the boil. Lower the heat, cover the pan and simmer gently for about 20 minutes, or until the lentils are just tender. Season to taste with salt and freshly ground pepper.

# CHICKEN AND PASTA BROTH
### Serves 4-6

*2 x 10 oz (300 g) chicken pieces*
*2 small leeks, sliced and washed*
*2 carrots, thinly sliced*
*1½ pts (900 ml) chicken stock*
*1 bouquet garni*
*salt and freshly ground pepper*
*2 oz (50 g) small pasta shapes*
*4 tbsp chopped parsley*

Put the chicken pieces in a large pan. Add the leeks and carrots and pour in the stock and 1½ pts (900 ml) water. Bring to the boil. Add the bouquet garni and salt and pepper, then lower the heat, cover the pan and simmer for 30 minutes until the chicken is tender. Remove the chicken from the liquid and put to one side until cool enough to handle. Meanwhile, add the pasta to the pan, bring back to the boil and simmer for 15 minutes, stirring occasionally, until the pasta is cooked. Remove the chicken from the bones and cut the flesh into bite size pieces, discarding all the skin. Return to the pan and heat through. Discard the bouquet garni and adjust seasoning. Serve hot in warmed soup bowls, each one sprinkled with chopped parsley.

# PARSNIP AND WALNUT SOUP
## Serves 4

*8 oz (225 g) parsnips, peeled and chopped*
*1 carrot, peeled and chopped*
*1 potato, peeled and chopped*
*1 onion, peeled and chopped*
*1 tbsp oil*
*1 pint (600 ml) water*
*½ pint (300 ml) milk*
*½ tsp ground nutmeg*
*salt and freshly ground black pepper*
*2 oz (50 g) walnuts, finely chopped*

Heat the oil in a large saucepan and fry the vegetables gently for a few minutes to seal, stirring frequently. Add the water and milk and cook gently for about 20 minutes until the vegetables are tender. Liquidise the soup in a food processor or blender and return to a clean saucepan, adding seasoning to taste. Thin the soup down with a little more milk if it is too thick. Re-heat gently and serve in individual bowls with the chopped walnuts sprinkled over the top of each portion.

# SWEET AND SOUR BEET AND CARAWAY SOUP
## Serves 6

*1 lb 2 oz (500 g) onion, finely chopped*
*2 oz (50 g) unsalted butter*
*1 clove garlic, finely chopped*
*2 tsp caraway seeds*
*3 tbsp dark brown sugar*
*1½ lb (675 g) beetroot, topped and coarsely grated*
*6 tbsp Balsamic vinegar*
*1½ pts (900 ml) chicken stock*
*plain Greek yoghurt and 6 parsley sprigs to garnish*

Melt the butter in a large saucepan and sauté the onion over a low heat until it is softened but not coloured. Add the garlic, caraway seeds and brown sugar and cook gently for about 3 minutes, stirring. Add the beetroot, vinegar, stock and about ¾ pint (450 ml) water and bring the mixture to the boil. Simmer the mixture, stirring occasionally, for about 20 minutes or until the beets are tender, adding salt and pepper to taste. Ladle the soup into 6 bowls and top each portion with about 2 tsp of the yoghurt and a parsley sprig.

## SAUSAGE AND POTATO SOUP
Serves 6

*2 large onions, chopped*
*4 large leeks, sliced*
*1/2 tsp caraway seeds*
*1/2 tsp nutmeg*
*1 oz (25 g) butter*
*2 lb (900 g) potatoes, diced*
*1 1/2 pts (900 ml) chicken stock*
*salt and freshly ground black pepper*
*8 oz (225 g) garlic or bierwurst sausage, diced*
*4 tbsp natural yoghurt*
*chopped parsley*

Sauté the onions, leeks and spices gently in the melted butter for 4 minutes, shaking the pan from time to time to ensure that the vegetables do not brown. Add the potatoes, stock and seasoning. Bring to the boil, cover the pan and simmer for 30 minutes or until the potato is tender. Add the sausage and yoghurt, stir well and garnish with chopped parsley. Serve with crusty bread and butter.

## SALMON AND POTATO SOUP
Serves 4

*1 onion, chopped*
*1 oz (25 g) butter*
*4 potatoes, parboiled and chopped*
*1 1/2 pts (900 ml) fish stock*
*1 lb (450 g) salmon fillet, cut into chunks*
*2 tbsp dill, chopped*
*salt and pepper*
*1/4 pt (150 ml) single cream*

Fry the onion in butter until soft. Add the potatoes, stock and salmon and bring to the boil. Simmer gently for 15 minutes, then add the dill, salt, pepper and cream.

# CHILLED SOUPS

## GAZPACHO
### Serves 4

*2 small onions, chopped*
*1 green pepper, cored, seeded and chopped*
*1 red pepper, cored, seeded and chopped*
*2 tomatoes, skinned, halved and seeded*
*1 pint (600 ml) tomato juice*
*2 garlic cloves, peeled*
*4 tbsp olive oil*
*salt*
*freshly ground black pepper*

*To serve:*
*4 tbsp fresh breadcrumbs*
*2 oz (50 g) butter*

Put the onion, peppers and tomato into a blender or food processor with the tomato juice, garlic and olive oil and season to taste. Blend until smooth. Chill for 3-4 hours. Fry the breadcrumbs in the butter until crisp. Drain on paper towels. Serve the fried crumbs sprinkled over the chilled soup.

## BORTSCH
### Serves 4

*6 small raw beetroot, about 2¼ lb (1 kg), peeled*
*2 medium onions, chopped*
*2 pts (1.1 litres) beef stock*
*salt and pepper*
*2 tbsp lemon juice*
*6 tbsp dry sherry*
*5 fl oz (150 ml) soured cream*
*chopped fresh chives to garnish*

Grate the beetroot coarsely and put it in a pan with the onion, stock and seasoning. Bring to the boil and simmer, covered, for 45 minutes. Strain, discard the vegetables and add the lemon juice and sherry to the liquid. Adjust seasoning. Serve well chilled with a whirl of soured cream and chopped chives.

## CHILLED PEA AND MINT SOUP
### Serves 6

*2 lb (900 g ) fresh peas, shelled*
*2 oz (50 g) margarine*
*1 onion, roughly chopped*
*1 pt (600 ml) milk*
*1 pt (600 ml) chicken stock*
*2 large sprigs of fresh mint and a few sprigs to garnish*
*pinch of caster sugar*
*salt and freshly ground pepper*
*5 fl oz (150 ml) single cream*

Melt the margarine in the saucepan, add the onion, cover and cook
gently for about 15 minutes until it is soft but not brown. Remove
from the heat and stir in the milk, stock, peas, mint sprigs, sugar and
seasoning. Bring to the boil, stirring. Cover and simmer gently for
about 30 minutes, until the peas are really tender. Cool slightly,
reserving 3 tbsp peas to garnish and rub the remaining peas through a
sieve or place in a blender or food processor and liquidise to form a
smooth puree. Pour into a large bowl. Adjust seasoning and cool. Stir
in the fresh cream and chill for 2-3 hours before serving. To serve,
garnish with the reserved boiled peas and sprigs of mint.

## CHILLED CUCUMBER AND WALNUT SOUP
### Serves 4

*2 medium cucumbers, peeled and diced*
*4 oz (110 g) walnuts, chopped*
*2 tbsp olive oil*
*1/2 pt (300 ml) chicken stock*
*1 clove garlic, crushed*
*2 tbsp fresh dill chopped or 2 tsp dried dill*
*salt and freshly ground pepper*
*1/2 pt (300 ml) natural yoghurt*
*sprigs of fresh dill to garnish*

Place the chopped cucumbers and walnuts in a bowl and add the oil,
stock, garlic and chopped dill and season to taste. Stir the soup well,
cover and chill in the refrigerator overnight. To serve, whisk in the
natural yoghurt and garnish with sprigs of dill.

## VICHYSSOISE
Serves 4-6

*3 medium leeks, cleaned*
*1 small onion, finely chopped*
*1 oz (25 g) butter*
*12 oz (350 g) potatoes, peeled and finely sliced*
*1 pt (600 ml) chicken stock*
*1 level tsp salt*
*freshly ground pepper*
*1 blade of mace*
*10 fl oz (300 ml) fresh double cream*
*2 tbsp snipped fresh chives or finely chopped watercress to garnish*

Finely chop the white part of the leeks. Melt the butter and add the leeks and onion and fry without browning for 7-10 minutes. Add the potatoes to the pan with the stock, salt, pepper and mace. Bring to the boil, then simmer for 20-30 minutes until the vegetables are tender. Sieve or blend and chill thoroughly. Just before serving stir in the fresh cream and serve sprinkled with chives or watercress.

## PRAWN AND AVOCADO SOUP
Serves 8

*2 large ripe avocados*
*2 tbsp lemon juice*
*1 pt (600 ml) chicken stock, cold*
*½ pt (300 ml) milk*
*salt and pepper*
*Worcestershire sauce*
*2½ fl oz (75 ml) mayonnaise*
*2½ fl oz (75 ml) single cream*
*1-2 tbsp tomato ketchup*
*2 oz (50 g) peeled prawns, chopped*
*1 level tsp chopped onion*

Mash together the lemon juice and avocado flesh. Whisk in the milk and stock and season with salt, pepper and Worcestershire sauce. Dilute with extra milk if the soup is too thick. Chill. Stir together the fresh cream and mayonnaise then blend in the tomato ketchup, chopped prawns, onion and Worcestershire sauce. Season. Serve the soup in bowls with a spoonful of swirled prawn sauce in each.

# CHILLED MUSHROOM AND LEMON SOUP
Serves 6-8

*1 lb (450 g) open mushrooms, wiped*
*grated rind and juice of 1 lemon*
*1 garlic clove, crushed*
*salt and pepper*
*1 level tsp dried thyme or 1 tbsp fresh thyme*
*1½ pts (900 ml) chicken stock*
*5 fl oz (150 ml) single cream*
*parsley sprigs to garnish*

Reserve a couple of mushrooms for garnish and roughly slice the remainder. Place in a flat dish and marinate with the lemon rind and juice, garlic, seasoning and herbs for several hours, turning occasionally. In a blender puree the mushrooms and the marinade with the stock. Stir in the fresh cream and adjust seasoning. Chill well before serving. Garnish with the remaining mushrooms, very finely sliced, and parsley sprigs.

# ICED TOMATO SOUP
Serves 4

*1 lb (450 g) ripe tomatoes*
*1 small onion, sliced*
*4 level tsp tomato puree*
*14½ oz (410 g) can chicken consommé*
*4 fresh basil leaves or 1 tsp dried basil*
*½ oz (10 g) fresh breadcrumbs*
*5 fl oz (150 ml) soured cream*

Roughly chop the tomatoes and liquidise them in a blender in two batches with the onion, tomato puree, consommé and basil. Rub through a sieve into a saucepan and heat gently to disperse the frothy texture. Season well. Add the breadcrumbs to the soup, and chill well before serving. Garnish with swirls of soured cream.

## MEDITERRANEAN SUMMER SOUP
Serves 4

*2 very large beef tomatoes*
*1 medium Spanish onion, skinned*
*1 green pepper, cored and seeded*
*1 lb (450 g) can potatoes, drained*
*4 cloves garlic, crushed*
*4 tbsp wine vinegar*
*1³/₄ pts (1 litre) water*
*2 tbsp olive oil*
*¹/₂ tsp paprika*
*salt and freshly ground pepper*
*fresh mint sprigs, to garnish*

Chop all the vegetables and put half of them together with the garlic in a blender with the vinegar and about ¼ pt (150 ml) of the measured water. Work to a smooth puree. Sieve the puree to remove the tomato skins, working it into a large soup tureen or bowl. Repeat this procedure with the remaining vegetables and another ¼ pt (150 ml) of the water. Add to the puree in the bowl. Put the remaining water into the soup and add the oil, paprika and seasoning to taste. Stir well to mix, cover and chill in the refrigerator for at least 1 hour before serving. To serve, taste and adjust the seasoning, then stir in ice cubes. Float mint sprigs on top. Serve as a starter for a summer luncheon or barbecue party with bowls of garnish such as tiny bread croutons, diced red and green pepper, diced cucumber and finely chopped hard-boiled eggs.

## ARTICHOKE SOUP (UNCOOKED)
Serves 4

*1 lb (450 g) Jerusalem artichokes*
*1 lb (450 g) potatoes*
*1 stick celery*
*1 pt (600 ml) milk*
*salt and pepper (or paprika)*
*1 tbsp chopped parsley*

Scrub the artichokes, potatoes and celery and grate them. Put the vegetables in a liquidiser with milk and seasoning and blend until smooth. Chill the soup and stir in the parsley just before serving. Eat as soon as possible.

## CHILLED WATERCRESS SOUP
Serves 4-6

*1 oz (25 g) butter*
*2 leeks, thinly sliced*
*1 small onion, chopped*
*8 oz (225 g) potato, diced*
*2 bunches of watercress*
*1 pint (600 ml) chicken stock*
*salt and pepper*
*1/2 pint (300 ml) milk*
*croutons to garnish*

Fry the leeks and onion in the butter for about 5 minutes without browning. Add the potato and cook for a further 3 minutes. Roughly chop the watercress leaves and add to the pan with the stock, and salt and pepper to taste. Bring to the boil, cover and simmer for 25-30 minutes. Sieve or blend until smooth. Add the milk and chill for several hours before serving. Serve garnished with croutons.

## CARROT AND ORANGE SOUP
Serves 6

*1 lb (450 g) carrots (sliced)*
*1 1/2 pts (900 ml) chicken stock*
*1 onion, chopped*
*pinch of sugar*
*salt and pepper*
*grated rind of one orange*
*juice of four oranges*
*1/4 pt (150 ml) single cream for garnish*
*4-6 orange slices for garnish*

Cook the carrots and onion in the melted butter for about 10 minutes without browning. Add the stock and sugar and season to taste. Bring to the boil, cover and simmer for about an hour or until the carrots are soft. Sieve or blend until smooth. Pour into a soup tureen and stir in the orange rind and juice. Cool and then chill for several hours. To serve, stir in the cream and garnish with orange slices.

## EASTERN AVOCADO SOUP
### Serves 6

*3 avocados, rather over-ripe*
*1¼ pts (750 ml) tomato juice*
*1½-3 tsp curry powder*
*2-3 tsp lemon juice*
*½ pt (300 ml) chicken stock*
*1 small carton natural yoghurt*
*½ pt (300 ml) cream*
*1 tbsp chopped chives or chopped nuts*
*lemon quarters*
*brown bread and butter or water biscuits for garnish*

Blend together in an electric blender the peeled and stoned avocados,
tomato juice, curry powder to taste and stock. When these ingredients
are blended, add the yoghurt, lemon juice, salt and pepper. Blend
again. Chill in the refrigerator until ready to serve and then stir in the
lightly whipped cream. Sprinkle with chopped chives or nuts and
serve with lemon quarters and brown bread and butter or water biscuits.

## CHILLED SUMMER SOUP
### Serves 6

*2 lb (900 g) peas, shelled*
*1 large bunch watercress*
*2 oz (50 g) butter*
*1 medium onion, skinned and thinly sliced*
*2 pts (1.1 ltr) milk*
*salt and pepper*
*5 fl oz (150 ml) fresh single cream*

Drain and roughly chop the well washed watercress, saving a few
sprigs for garnish. Cook the onion and watercress in melted butter in
a saucepan for about 15 minutes, without browning. Remove from
the heat and stir in the milk, peas and seasoning. Bring to the boil,
stirring. Cover and simmer gently for about 30 minutes, until the peas
are soft. Cool slightly, rub through a sieve or puree in a blender.
Adjust seasoning and cool. Stir in the cream and chill well before
serving, garnished with watercress sprigs.

## COLD CHERRY SOUP
### Serves 6

*8 oz (225 g) caster sugar*
*1 cinnamon stick*
*1½ pts (900 ml) plus 2 tbsp water*
*1 lb 2 oz (500 g) fresh morello cherries, stoned or canned cherries, drained*
*6 fl oz (180 ml) dry red wine*
*1 tbsp arrowroot*
*4 tbsp soured cream, to serve (optional)*

Dissolve the sugar in 1½ pints (900 ml) of the water in a saucepan with the cinnamon added, over a low heat. Bring to the boil and boil gently for 5 minutes. Chop the cherries and add to the pan. Bring the syrup back to the boil and simmer for 30 minutes (only simmer for 10 minutes if using canned cherries). Remove the cinnamon and stir in the wine. Make a paste of the arrowroot with the rest of the water and stir in a little of the syrup. Add the mixture to the saucepan and bring to the boil, stirring constantly. Simmer for 2-3 minutes or until clear and thickened. Cool and chill. To serve, swirl the soured cream on top if using.

## CRANBERRY AND ORANGE SOUP
### Serves 4-6

*1 lb (450 g) fresh cranberries (or canned equivalent)*
*¾ pt (450 ml) light chicken stock (or water)*
*12 fl oz (350 ml) white wine*
*2-3 pieces lemon rind*
*pared rind of a ripe orange*
*½ cinnamon stick*
*2-4 oz (50-110 g) sugar to taste*
*juice of two oranges*
*juice of half lemon*
*4-6 orange slices for garnish*

Wash the cranberries if fresh. Put them in a pan with the chicken stock (or water) and white wine. Add the pieces of lemon and orange rind and cinnamon stick. Simmer for about 10 minutes, until the cranberries are soft. Remove the cinnamon stick and sieve the fruit and juice. Sweeten to taste and add the orange and lemon juice (if using canned cranberries it may not be necessary to add any sugar as these are usually sweetened). Serve chilled with a thin slice of orange to garnish.

# ICED AVOCADO SOUP
### Serves 6

*2-3 ripe avocados*
*3 tsp lemon juice*
*1 tsp onion juice*
*dash of Tabasco sauce*
*1¼ pts (750 ml) chicken stock*
*1 small carton natural yoghurt*
*1 large pinch grated nutmeg*
*½ pt (300 ml) double cream*
*1-2 level tsp fresh chopped dill or a few fresh tarragon leaves*

Peel the avocados and mash the flesh, reserving a quarter of one avocado to use as a garnish. Sprinkle this reserved quarter with lemon juice and wrap in clingfilm until required. Stir the rest of the lemon juice into the mashed avocado flesh. Add a dash of Tabasco and onion juice made by crushing a small piece of onion in a garlic press or squeezing through a fine sieve. Blend all these ingredients together in an electric blender, adding the stock a little at a time. Add the natural yoghurt together with seasoning and nutmeg and blend again. Fold in half the cream leaving the soup with a marbled appearance. Pour into soup cups and chill. Just before serving whip the remaining cream lightly and cut the reserved ¼ avocado into thin slivers. Put a spoonful of whipped cream into each cup and top with a slice or two of avocado. Dust with a small amount of paprika.

# CHILLED COURGETTE SOUP
### Serves 3-4

*1½ oz (35 g) butter*
*1 lb (450 g) courgettes, sliced*
*15 oz (425 g) can consommé*
*half bunch watercress*
*salt*
*freshly ground black pepper*
*¼ pt (150 ml) natural yoghurt*

Melt the butter in a pan and add the courgettes. Cover and cook gently for 5 minutes, then stir in the consommé and bring to the boil. Trim off the thick watercress stalks and add the leaves to the pan with the seasoning. Cover and simmer for 20 minutes. Puree or sieve then chill thoroughly. When ready to serve, stir in the yoghurt.

# ICED AVOCADO AND CHICKEN SOUP
### Serves 6

*2 ripe avocados*
*1 small onion, chopped*
*finely grated rind and juice of 1 lemon*
*5 fl oz (150 ml) natural yoghurt*
*5 fl oz (150 ml) soured cream*
*1 pt (600 ml) cold chicken stock*
*6 oz (175 g) cooked chicken, diced*
*salt and freshly ground pepper*
*snipped chives to garnish*

Halve the avocados and discard the stones. Scoop out the flesh with a teaspoon. Liquidise the avocado flesh, onion, lemon rind and juice, yoghurt and soured cream in a blender or food processor. Turn into a large serving bowl or tureen, gradually whisk in the stock, then add the chicken and season to taste. Cover tightly and chill for at least 2 hours. To garnish, snip chives over the surface of the soup just before serving.

# JELLIED GAZPACHO
### Serves 6

*1 beef stock cube*
*3/4 pt (450 ml) boiling water*
*3/4 pt (450 ml) tomato juice*
*1/2 oz (10 g) gelatine*
*2 tomatoes, peeled, seeded and chopped*
*1 small onion, chopped*
*half cucumber, peeled, seeded and chopped*
*2 tbsp vegetable oil*
*2 tbsp white wine vinegar*

Dissolve the stock cube in boiling water. Put into a pan with the tomato juice and gelatine and heat gently until the gelatine has dissolved. Leave to cool. Mix the chopped vegetables with the oil and vinegar, season well and leave until the gelatine liquid is almost set. When it begins to set, pour the gelatine liquid through a fine sieve onto the vegetables and chill until completely set.

# BARCELONA SOUP
Serves 4

*1 lb (450 g) very ripe tomatoes, peeled and seeded*
*1 large clove garlic, chopped*
*1 lb (450 g) cucumber, peeled and seeded*
*1 large egg*
*6 fl oz (180 ml) olive oil*
*2 tsp Balsamic vinegar*

Chop the cucumber into 1 inch (2.5 cm) pieces. Put the cucumber, tomatoes and garlic into a blender or food processor and liquidise. Transfer the mixture to a bowl. In the blender blend the egg with a pinch of salt until it is smooth and, with the motor running, add the oil in a stream, blending until the mixture is the consistency of mayonnaise. Add the tomato mixture, 2½ fl oz (75 ml) water, the vinegar and salt and pepper to taste and blend until smooth. Transfer the soup to a bowl and chill it, covered, overnight to let the flavours develop.

# MEAT AND POULTRY

## HAM AND CHEESE CUPS
Makes around 30 cups

*Cheese pastry:*
*3 oz (75 g) lard*
*3 oz (75 g) hard margarine*
*12 oz (350 g) plain flour*
*4 oz (110 g) grated cheese*
*pinch mustard powder*
*pinch cayenne pepper*
*pinch salt*

*Filling:*
*1 tbsp butter, melted*
*6 oz (175 g) cooked ham, finely chopped*
*3 eggs*
*6-8 fl oz (180-240 ml) single cream*
*4 oz (110g) Gruyère cheese, grated*

Preheat the oven to 400°F/200°C/Gas Mk 6. Sieve the flour, salt, mustard and cayenne pepper together and lightly rub in the lard and margarine until the mixture resembles fine breadcrumbs. Stir in the grated cheese. Gradually stir in enough cold water (about 4 tbsp) to make a smooth dough, which leaves the sides of the bowl clean. Roll out the dough on a floured surface to about ⅛ inch (4 mm) thick. Using a 3 inch (7.5 cm) fluted cutter, cut the pastry into rounds. Line a muffin or small cup-cake tin with the pastry circles, brush with melted butter, cover and refrigerate until ready to fill. Beat together the eggs and cream until well blended. Season. Sprinkle some of the diced ham and Gruyère cheese into each cup. Spoon about 1 tbsp of the egg mixture into each pastry cup. Bake in the oven for 20 minutes until the custard has set. Remove from the tin and serve immediately.

# QUICHE LORRAINE
Serves 6-8

*6 oz (175 g) shortcrust pastry*
*6 oz (175 g) streaky bacon, derinded and chopped*
*2 eggs*
*2 egg yolks*
*¼ pint (150 ml) single cream*
*¼ pint (150 ml) milk*
*2 oz (50 g) Gruyère cheese, grated*
*salt and freshly ground black pepper*

*Oven: 190°C/375°F/Gas Mk 5*

Roll out the pastry and line an 8 inch (20 cm) flan tin or ring. Bake blind. Lower the heat to 180°C/350°F/Gas Mk 4. Sauté the bacon gently in its own fat until brown. Put the bacon into the prepared flan case. Beat together the eggs, cream and milk and season to taste. Pour into the prepared flan case and sprinkle with the cheese. Bake for 25-30 minutes until set and golden. Serve hot or cold.

# BRATWURST WITH LENTILS
Serves 4

*1 lb (450 g) bratwurst sausages*
*2 tbsp polyunsaturated oil*
*8 oz (225 g) onions*
*6 oz (175 g) no-soak American or red lentils*
*½ level tsp dried thyme*
*2 bay leaves*
*¾-1 pint (450-600 ml) seasoned stock*
*mild mustard*

*Oven: 325°F/170°C/Gas Mk 3*

Brown the sausages in hot oil in a large flameproof casserole. Remove them, then lightly fry the sliced onions. Chop the sausages into bite-sized pieces. Add the lentils, thyme, bay leaves and stock to the onions in the casserole. Place the sausages on top and bring to the boil. Cover. Place in the oven and bake for about 30 minutes. Stir in mustard to taste. Serve with crusty French bread and beer.

# KOFTA
Serves 5 (4 cocktail sticks per person).

*Meatballs:*
*1 lb (450 g) lean minced lamb*
*1 tbsp freshly chopped mint*
*2 tbsp freshly chopped parsley*
*1 tsp ground cumin*
*1 tsp ground coriander*
*5 cardamom pods, shelled and seeds crushed*
*salt and black pepper*

*Mint Yoghurt:*
*2 x 5 oz (150 g) cartons natural yoghurt*
*juice of 1 lemon*
*1 clove garlic, crushed*
*1 tbsp freshly chopped mint*
*1 tbsp freshly chopped coriander*

Pound together all the meatball ingredients and shape into 40 little balls. Thread onto cocktail sticks, two per stick. Chill. Mix together all the mint yoghurt ingredients to make a dip. Pour into a serving bowl. Just before serving, grill the meatballs for 10-15 minutes until they are cooked through. Serve warm with the dip.

# MINI EGG AND BACON QUICHES
Serves 6

*8 oz (225 g) prepared shortcrust pastry*

*Filling:*
*5 eggs, beaten*
*1/3 pt (200 ml) single cream*
*6 oz (175 g) lean bacon, derinded and diced*
*4 spring onions, chopped*
*a little grated nutmeg*
*salt and freshly ground pepper*

Line six 4 inch (10 cm) tins with pastry. Mix together the eggs, cream, nutmeg and pepper to taste. Divide the bacon between the pastry cases. Sprinkle with spring onions and pour in the egg mixture. Bake in a preheated moderate oven for 25 minutes, until golden brown. Remove from the tins and serve hot or cold with a side salad.

# HAM AND ASPARAGUS ROLLS
Serves 4

*4 large slices cooked ham*
*1 can asparagus*
*salt and freshly ground black pepper*

*Sauce:*
*1½ oz (35 g) butter*
*1½ oz (35 g) flour*
*¾ pt (450 ml) milk*
*small glass white wine*
*3 oz (75 g) Cheddar cheese, grated*
*½ tsp mustard*
*salt and pepper*

*Oven: 350°F/180°C/Gas Mk 4*

Drain the asparagus and divide between the 4 slices of ham. Roll up with the asparagus in the middle. Place in an ovenproof dish. Melt the butter in a pan and stir in the flour. Cook for a few minutes stirring all the time. Gradually add the milk, bring to the boil and simmer gently until the sauce has thickened. Add the wine, cheese and mustard and continue cooking for another 3 minutes. Pour over the ham and asparagus and bake for 15 minutes.

# SALAMI WITH AVOCADO AND GRAPEFRUIT
Serves 4

*1 large, ripe avocado*
*1 large, pink grapefruit*
*8 slices salami*
*French dressing*
*mint sprigs*

Peel and segment the grapefruit, removing all the pith. Peel and halve the avocado, and cut into slices. This should be prepared at the very last minute to prevent the flesh from turning brown. Alternate the avocado slices with the pink grapefruit segments on one side of each serving plate. Place two slices of salami in the remaining space. Garnish each plate with a sprig of mint and serve the French dressing separately.

# SWISS BACON AND MUSHROOM TOASTS
Serves 6

*12 thin slices white bread*
*8 oz (225 g) grated Swiss cheese*
*¼ pt (150 ml) double cream*
*4 eggs*
*¼ pt (150 ml) milk*
*8 tbsp butter*

*Filling:*
*12 slices bacon*
*12-14 mushrooms*
*2 tbsp butter*
*2 tbsp lemon juice*

Trim the crusts from the bread. Mix the Swiss cheese and cream, and spread on all the bread slices. Spread the filling (see below) onto half the bread slices and top with the remaining slices, cheese side down. Beat the eggs and milk with a fork. Dip the sandwiches into the egg mixture, coating both sides. Heat the butter in a large frying pan and brown the sandwiches on both sides over a moderate heat. Serve with a knife and fork or cut into bite-sized pieces.

Filling: for 6 sandwiches, use 12 slices bacon, and 12-14 finely sliced mushrooms sautéed in 2 tbsp each of butter and lemon juice. Fry the bacon over moderate heat. Drain on paper towels. Use about 1 tbsp mushrooms and 2 slices of bacon to fill each sandwich.

## LITTLE PROVENCALE TARTLETS
Makes 12

*1 lb (450 g) shortcrust pastry*
*8 anchovy fillets, finely chopped*
*1 small onion, finely chopped*
*1 clove garlic, finely chopped*
*2-4 tbsp olive oil*
*2 tbsp finely chopped parsley*
*8 oz (225 g) cooked ham or veal, finely chopped*
*1-2 egg yolks*
*salt and freshly ground black pepper*

Prepare the shortcrust pastry. Cut out 24 small circles of dough with a biscuit cutter. Pound the finely chopped anchovy fillets, onion and garlic to a smooth paste in a mortar with olive oil. Blend in the finely chopped parsley, ham or veal, and 1 or 2 egg yolks - the mixture must not be too wet. Season to taste with salt and freshly ground black pepper. Place 1 tbsp of this mixture in the centre of 12 of the pastry rounds, wet the edges of the dough and cover with the remaining pastry rounds, pressing the edges together firmly. Brush with egg yolk and bake in a moderate oven (375°F/190°C/Gas Mk 5) for about 20 minutes or until the crust is golden.

## FRUITY HAM CORNETS
Serves 4

*3 oz (75 g) cream cheese*
*1 oz (25 g) mayonnaise*
*1 small can crushed pineapple (well drained)*
*1 oz (25 g) sultanas*
*4 thin slices ham*

Blend together the cheese and mayonnaise. Stir in all the other ingredients except the ham. Season the mixture, divide between the ham slices and roll up to form cornet shapes. Place on a serving dish.

## SAVOURY VOL-AU-VENTS
Serves 5

*2 x 14 oz (400 g) pkts frozen puff pastry, thawed*
*beaten egg to glaze*

*Oven: 450°F/230°C/Gas Mk 8*

Roll out each packet of pastry to an oblong 9 x 9½ inches
(23 x 24.5 cm) and using a 3 inch (7.5 cm) round plain cutter, cut out
five rounds from each packet. Place on dampened baking sheets and
brush with beaten egg. Using a 2 inch (5 cm) round plain cutter, cut
part-way through the centre of each round. Bake in the oven for
about 20 minutes until well risen and golden. Remove the soft centres
from each vol-au-vent and cool the cases on a wire rack. Before serving, fill with your preferred cold filling and reheat in the oven at
350°F/180°C/Gas Mk 4 for about 15 minutes.

## SPICED BACON AND CELERY
## VOL-AU-VENT FILLING
Serves 10

*1 lb (450 g) smoked bacon, chopped into small pieces*
*6 oz (175 g) celery, cleaned, trimmed and cut into 1 in (2.5 cm) pieces*
*1½ oz (35 g) butter*
*¼ tsp ground ginger*
*¼ tsp ground cumin*
*¼ tsp ground coriander*
*1½ oz (35 g) flour*
*¾ pt (450 ml) chicken stock*
*½ tbsp tomato puree*
*2½ oz (60 g) natural yoghurt*
*1 tbsp parsley, chopped*
*salt and freshly ground black pepper*

Melt the butter in a saucepan and gently cook the bacon for 1 minute.
Remove and keep on one side. Add the celery to the juices in the pan
and sauté together with the spices for 5 minutes. Stir in the flour and
cook gently for 1-2 minutes, stirring. Remove from the heat and gradually stir in the stock, tomato puree, yoghurt and parsley. Return to
the heat and bring to the boil, then simmer for 4-5 minutes, stirring all
the time. Now add the bacon pieces and season to taste. Cool the
mixture before filling the vol-au-vent cases and then reheat.

# CROQUE MONSIEUR
Serves 4

*8 slices Gruyère cheese*
*4 slices ham*
*8 slices white bread, buttered*
*1 egg, beaten*
*fresh breadcrumbs for coating*
*oil for shallow frying*

Arrange the cheese and ham slices alternately on 4 slices of bread. Top with the remaining bread, pressing the sandwich together. Coat with beaten egg and breadcrumbs. Heat the oil in a frying pan and fry, two sandwiches at a time, until golden brown. Drain on kitchen paper. Cut in half and serve immediately.

# POTTED BEEF
Serves 6

*1 lb (450 g) stewing steak, cut into 1/2 inch (1.25 cm) cubes*
*1/4 pint (150 ml) stock*
*1 clove*
*1 blade of mace*
*salt and pepper*
*2 oz (50 g) butter*
*fresh bay leaves for garnish*

*Oven: 350°F/180°C/Gas Mk 4*

Put the meat in a casserole with the stock and seasonings and cover with a lid. Place in the centre of a preheated oven and cook for about 3 hours or until the meat is very tender. Remove the clove and mace and drain off the stock into another bowl. Reserve the stock. Place the meat in a food processor or blender and liquidise until smooth. Add 1 oz (25 g) melted butter and enough of the reserved stock to moisten. Press into individual ramekins or cocotte dishes, level the top and cover with the remaining melted butter. Serve garnished with a fresh bay leaf on top of each with hot toast fingers.

# OLD ENGLAND STARTER
### Serves 4

*4-8 slices (depending on size) cold roast beef*

*Red cabbage slaw:*
*4 oz (110 g) red cabbage*
*3 fl oz (90 ml) sour cream*
*1 tsp horseradish cream*
*1 clove garlic, crushed*
*salt*
*freshly ground black pepper*
*1 tsp white wine vinegar*
*1 tbsp finely chopped parsley*

Shred the cabbage very finely and place in a bowl. Mix all the remaining ingredients (except the roast beef) together and pour over the cabbage. Toss lightly with two forks. Chill. Place one or two rolled slices of roast beef on an individual serving plate and place a pile of red cabbage slaw next to it. Sprinkle the slaw with chopped parsley and hand round horseradish sauce separately.

# HONEYED KEBABS WITH APPLE
### Serves 4

*2 tbsp soy sauce*
*5 tbsp honey*
*1 level tsp ground ginger*
*juice of half lemon*
*1 lb (450 g) boneless pork, cut into 1 in (2.5 cm) cubes*
*1 large green pepper, cut into squares*
*4 small onions, halved*
*2 apples, quartered and cored*
*8 medium-sized mushrooms*

Combine the soy sauce, honey, ground ginger and lemon juice in a large bowl. Add the pork cubes to the marinade and leave to marinate for 3-4 hours or overnight. Thread the meat onto 4 skewers, alternating with pieces of green pepper, onion, apple and the mushrooms. Place the kebabs under a hot grill, turning frequently until cooked through. Baste with the remaining marinade.

# INDONESIAN PORK SATAY
Serves 4

*1 lb (450 g) pork fillet*
*2 tbsp dark soy sauce*
*3 tbsp lemon juice*
*1½ tsp ground ginger*
*4 oz (110 g) unsalted peanuts*
*1 garlic clove, skinned and crushed*
*½ tsp ground coriander*
*¼ tsp chilli powder*
*¼ tsp salt*
*¾ pint (450 ml) coconut milk*
*1 tsp soft brown sugar*
*freshly ground pepper*
*half cucumber, shredded*

Cut the pork fillet into small cubes. Thread onto 8 long satay sticks, or metal skewers. Mix together the soy sauce, lemon juice and 1 tsp of the ginger. Pour over the pork and leave to marinate for about 30 minutes, turning occasionally. Meanwhile finely chop the peanuts or grind them. Add the peanuts, garlic, coriander, chilli powder, remaining ginger and salt and fry in a little oil for about 4-5 minutes until browned, stirring. Stir in the coconut milk and sugar. Bring to the boil and simmer for about 15 minutes until the sauce thickens. Check the seasoning, adding pepper to taste. Grill the meat for about 6 minutes, until it is tender, turning occasionally. Serve the satay hot, with the cucumber and the peanut sauce for dipping.

# GRILLED AUBERGINE AND HAM
Serves 4

*2 large aubergines*
*salt*
*olive oil*
*French dressing*
*chopped chives*
*1 large slice Parma ham per person*

Wipe the aubergine, trim and cut into slices about ½ inch (1.25 cm) thick. Place in a shallow dish and sprinkle well with salt. Leave for half an hour, then rinse and wipe dry with kitchen paper. Soak the slices in olive oil and then place under a hot grill, turning once. Sprinkle with French dressing and chopped chives. Serve cold with slices of ham.

## AMERICAN SPARE RIBS
Serves 4

*12 oz (350 g) onions, chopped*
*2 cloves of garlic, crushed*
*4 tbsp vinegar*
*2½ oz (60 g) can of tomato puree*
*¼ tsp chilli powder*
*6 tbsp clear honey*
*2 beef stock cubes, crumbled*
*½ pint (300 ml) water*
*2½ lb (1.1 kg) pork ribs*
*salt & pepper*

*Oven: 375°F/190°C/Gas Mk 5*

Heat 2 tbsp oil in a large saucepan, add the onions and fry gently for about 15 minutes or until pale golden brown and soft. Add all the remaining ingredients except the ribs and bring to the boil, stirring constantly. Simmer uncovered for 10 minutes. Arrange the ribs in a single layer in a shallow heatproof dish, season with salt and pepper and pour over half the sauce. Cook in the oven for 45 minutes. Remove from the oven and drain off the surplus fat or oil or blot with kitchen paaper. Coat with the remaining sauce and roast for a further 15-30 minutes or until golden brown and tender.

## ITALIAN HAM AND MELON STARTER
Serves 4-6

*1 Ogen or Galia melon*
*1 Honeydew melon*
*4 oz (110 g) Italian salami*
*4 oz (110 g) Parma ham*
*4 oz (110 g) mild Cheddar or Lancashire cheese*

Leave the melons to stand at room temperature for 30 minutes, then cut into quarters, lengthwise. Scoop out the seeds and discard. Run a thin bladed knife closely between the flesh and the rind until they separate. Place the flesh back on the rind and cut the Ogen quarters into four slices and the honeydew slices into six slices. Place the sliced melons alternately on a large platter and fan out the wedges. Arrange slices of salami and Parma ham between the melon wedges, folded in fan shapes. Slice the cheese as thinly as possible and place in the centre of the plate. Season generously with freshly ground black pepper and serve with crusty French bread.

# CHEESE AND HAM AIGRETTES
Makes about 20

*1 oz (25 g) butter*
*2 oz (50 g) flour*
*2 eggs*
*1 oz (25 g) Cheddar cheese, grated*
*1 oz (25 g) ham, finely chopped*
*1 tsp finely chopped onion*
*salt*
*cayenne pepper*
*oil for deep-frying*

Bring the butter and 4 tbsp water to boiling point, and remove from the heat. Add the flour all at once stirring quickly until the mixture forms a soft ball and leaves the sides of the pan clean. Cool slightly. Gradually add the eggs, beating them in until the mixture is smooth, shiny and firm enough to stand in soft peaks. Add the cheese, ham, onion and seasonings. Mix well. Drop small teaspoonfuls of the mixture into hot oil and fry each for about 4-5 minutes until golden brown. Serve at once sprinkled with the cayenne pepper.

# HAM AND CELERY MADEIRA
Serves 4

*4 large slices of cooked ham*
*2 canned celery hearts*
*1 oz (25 g) butter*
*3 tbsp tomato soup*
*½ tsp paprika*
*pinch ground mace*
*½ pt (300 ml) water*
*2 tbsp red wine*
*chopped parsley*

*Oven: 350°F/180°C/Gas Mk 4*

Cut the celery hearts in half lengthwise and wrap a slice of ham round each. Arrange in the bottom of a fireproof dish. Melt the butter in a pan and add the tomato soup, paprika and ground mace and cook for 1 minute. Add the water and red wine and bring to boiling point, stirring. Pour over the rolls of ham and heat through in a moderate oven for 15-20 minutes. Garnish with chopped parsley before serving.

# BEEF KEBABS WITH HORSERADISH DIP

Serves 4

*3 fl oz (90 ml) whipping cream*
*¹/₄ pint (150 ml) soured cream*
*2 tbsp grated fresh horseradish*
*1 tsp white wine vinegar*
*¹/₂ tsp sugar*
*1 lb (450 g) minced beef*
*1 small onion, skinned and grated*
*1 oz (25 g) fresh white or brown breadcrumbs*
*2 tbsp chopped fresh coriander or parsley*
*2 tsp ground cumin*
*¹/₄ tsp cayenne pepper*
*1 tsp salt*
*1 egg, beaten*
*8 cherry tomatoes, or 2 tomatoes, quartered*
*12 bay leaves*

To make the dip whip the creams together, then fold in the horseradish, vinegar and sugar. Season, then chill in the refrigerator. Mix together the minced beef, onion, breadcrumbs, coriander, cumin, cayenne and salt until they are all combined. Bind with the egg. With wet hands, form the mixture into 16 balls. Thread 4 balls on each of 4 oiled kebab skewers, alternating with tomatoes and bay leaves. Brush the kebabs with oil, then grill under a preheated moderate grill for 10 minutes, turning frequently and brushing with oil so that they cook evenly. Serve the beef kebabs hot on individual plates. Serve the horseradish dip separately.

# CHICKEN SPINACH PARCELS
## Serves 6

*6 boned and skinned chicken breasts*
*8 oz (225 g) fresh spinach*
*nutmeg*
*tomato sauce*

*Oven: 350°F/180°C/Gas Mk 4*

Blanch the spinach in boiling water for about 1 minute. Remove and separate the leaves to drain. Sprinkle the chicken breasts with a small amount of nutmeg and wrap each piece in spinach leaves. Place in a lighly-oiled ovenproof dish and cover with tomato sauce to taste. Cook in the oven for 30 minutes.

# LAMB BROCHETTES
## Serves 4

*1 lb (450 g) lamb, cubed*
*2 courgettes, wiped and sliced*
*8 shallots, peeled and halved*

*Marinade:*
*1 tbsp soy sauce*
*1 clove of garlic, peeled and crushed*
*1 tbsp wholegrain mustard*
*2 tbsp clear honey*

*Dip:*
*¼ pint (150 ml) soured cream*
*2 tsp wholegrain mustard*
*1 tsp clear honey*

Mix all the marinade ingredients together. Place the meat and vegetables in a shallow dish and pour the marinade over, turning with a slotted spoon to make sure the ingredients are completely coated. Cover and place in the refrigerator for at least 1 hour. Mix all the ingredients for the dip together and place in a serving dish. Chill. When ready to cook thread the meat and vegetables alternately on to 8 skewers, allowing three pieces of meat to a skewer. Brush with the marinade and grill under a preheated grill for 15-20 minutes, turning regularly and basting with the marinade. Serve immediately with the dip.

## SATAY KAMBING
Serves 4-6

*2 lb (1 kg) boned breast of lamb*
*¼ pint (150 ml) cider vinegar*
*1 onion, grated*
*2 cloves garlic, crushed*
*2 level tsp salt*
*½ level tsp chilli powder*
*2 level tsp ground coriander*
*1 level tsp ground cumin*
*½ level tsp turmeric*
*1 level tsp ground ginger*

Cut the lamb into ½ in (1.25 cm) cubes and put into a bowl. Stir in the vinegar and put aside for 30 minutes. Drain. Mix together the onion, garlic, salt, chilli powder, coriander, cumin, turmeric and ground ginger in a large bowl. Add to the lamb, coat well and leave for a further 30 minutes. Thread the pieces of meat onto 4-6 skewers. Place under a hot grill for 10-15 minutes, or until cooked through, turning frequently.

## CHICKEN STUFFED APPLES
Serves 4

*8 oz (225 g) cooked chicken*
*5 fl oz (150 ml) natural yoghurt*
*1 small carton of cottage cheese*
*2 oz (50 g) white seedless grapes, peeled*
*2 celery stalks, chopped*
*4 large apples*
*1 oz (25 g) flaked almonds*
*grated rind of half lemon*
*salt and pepper*

Chop the chicken into small pieces and mix with the grapes and celery. Stir in the yoghurt and cottage cheese and mix well. Wash and polish the apples and cut in half. Remove the cores and scoop out the flesh leaving a good shape of apple skins. Chop the apple flesh and mix in with the chicken. Add salt and pepper to taste and replace the mixture in the apple skins. Sprinkle the tops with almonds and lemon rind.

## CHICKEN AND HAM CROQUETTES
Serves 8

*1 whole chicken breast, cooked and finely minced*
*1 very small onion, finely minced*
*¼ tsp thyme*
*3 tbsp butter*
*5 tbsp olive oil*
*5 oz (150 g) flour*
*12 fl oz (360 ml) milk*
*4 fl oz (120 ml) strong chicken stock*
*salt and freshly ground pepper*
*good pinch of nutmeg*
*2½ oz (60 g) ham, finely minced*
*2 eggs, lightly beaten with 2 tsp water*
*bread crumbs*

Heat the butter and olive oil and sauté the onion gently until soft but not brown. Add the flour and cook for 3 minutes, stirring constantly. Gradually add the milk, stock and seasonings and cook gently, stirring constantly, until a thick, smooth sauce is obtained. Add the minced chicken and ham and continue cooking and stirring for another 10 minutes, until the sauce reaches boiling point. Leave to cool in a flat dish. Refrigerate. When ready to use, divide the mixture into 1 inch (2.5 cm) balls with floured hands. Dip the croquettes in beaten egg and coat with the bread crumbs. Refrigerate again for at least 1 hour. Fry quickly in hot oil until golden. Drain and serve with a side salad.

## DEVILLED DRUMSTICKS
Serves 6

*2 oz (50 g) butter*
*1 level tbsp demerara sugar*
*2 level tsp French mustard*
*½ level tsp salt*
*12 chicken drumsticks*

*Oven: 375°F/190°C/Gas Mk 5*

Melt the butter and add it to the sugar, mustard and salt. Place the drumsticks in a mixing bowl and pour over the butter mixture, turning the drumsticks to coat evenly. When the butter glaze has set, wrap each drumstick separately in foil. Place on a baking sheet and cook in the oven for 1 hour. Open the foil for the last 20 minutes to brown.

## SPICY LAMB KEBABS
Makes 8

*1½ lb (675 g) boned leg of lamb*
*1 lb (450 g) courgettes*
*8 tomatoes, halved*
*1 large corn on the cob*
*8 shallots*
*5 oz (150 g) natural yoghurt*
*1 garlic clove, crushed*
*2 bay leaves, crumbled*
*1 tbsp lemon juice*
*1 tbsp vegetable oil*
*1 tsp ground allspice*
*1 tbsp coriander seeds*
*freshly ground pepper*
*lemon wedges, to garnish*

Cut the lamb into 1 inch (2.5 cm) cubes. Slice courgettes thickly. Cut the corn into eight slices and blanch in boiling salted water. Drain well and set aside. Blanch the shallots in boiling, salted water, skin and set aside. Pour the yoghurt into a shallow dish. Stir in the garlic, bay leaves, lemon juice, oil, allspice and coriander seeds. Season. Thread the lamb cubes onto eight skewers with all the vegetables. Place in a dish and spoon over the marinade. Cover and leave for 2-3 hours. Cook the kebabs for 15-20 minutes under the grill or on a barbecue, turning and brushing with marinade occasionally.

## TANGY LEMON CHICKEN WINGS
Serves 4

*12 chicken wings*
*juice and rind of 2 lemons*
*4 oz (110 g) fresh breadcrumbs*
*½ tsp paprika*
*salt and pepper*

*Oven: 200°C/400°F/Gas Mk 6*

Cut off the tips of the chicken wings and discard. Put the wings into a shallow dish and pour over the lemon juice. Set aside for 1 hour. Mix the breadcrumbs with the lemon rind and paprika, and season. Toss each wing in the mixture, making sure that it is completely coated. Place the wings on a baking tray and cook for 25-30 minutes until they are golden and crisp.Serve with a tomato or garlic dip.

# SHASHLIK
## Serves 4

*1¹/₂-2 lb (675-900g) boneless lamb, trimmed of fat*
*5 tbsp red wine vinegar*
*6 tbsp olive oil*
*2 tsp grated nutmeg*
*2 tsp dried marjoram*
*salt and pepper*
*8 thick rashers of streaky bacon*
*4 small onions, skinned*
*16 bay leaves*

Cube the lamb. Place the wine vinegar, oil, nutmeg and marjoram in a bowl with lots of pepper. Whisk with a fork until well combined, then add the cubed lamb and stir to coat in the marinade. Cover and chill overnight. When ready to cook, cut each bacon rasher into 4-6 pieces, discarding the rind. Cut the onions into eighths. Thread the lamb, bacon, onions and bay leaves onto 8 oiled kebab skewers. Cook over a charcoal barbecue or under the grill for about 15 minutes until the lamb is tender but still pink and juicy on the inside. Turn the skewers frequently during cooking and baste with any remaining marinade or olive oil. Sprinkle with salt and pepper to taste before serving. Serve on a bed of rice or with warmed pitta bread.

# CHICKEN LIVER EN SURPRISE
## Serves 4

*4 chicken livers*
*1 oz (25 g) butter*
*salt and freshly ground black pepper*
*3 tbsp Cheddar cheese, grated*
*2 tbsp double cream*
*4 oz (110 g) well creamed, mashed potato*
*paprika*

*Oven: 400°F/200°C/Gas Mk 6*

Sauté the livers very gently in the butter for 3 minutes. Put 1 liver in each of 4 small ovenproof dishes and pour the melted butter and juices over each. Season. Top with 2 tbsp of the cheese, the cream, and a thin coating of the creamed potato. This looks better if it is piped in ribbons over the top. Sprinkle the remainder of the cheese on top and bake for a further 10-15 minutes. Serve sprinkled with paprika.

## ORIENTAL SPARE RIBS
Serves 4

*grated rind and juice of 1 large orange*
*3 tbsp vinegar*
*1 tbsp Worcestershire sauce*
*2 oz (50 g) soft brown sugar*
*2 lb (900 g) Chinese spare ribs*
*1 oz (25 g) butter*
*2 lb (900 g) white cabbage, finely shredded*
*1 lb (450 g) carrots, finely sliced*
*1 level tsp salt*

*Oven: 190°C/375°F/Gas Mk 5*

Place the orange rind and juice, vinegar, Worcestershire sauce and brown sugar in a bowl and stir well. Put the spare ribs in a shallow dish and pour over the marinade. Turn the ribs to coat them thoroughly and leave for 3-4 hours. Melt the butter in a large saucepan, add the juice from the marinade and the cabbage and carrots. Season and bring to the boil, then lower the heat and simmer for 10 minutes. Turn into a casserole dish, place the spare ribs on top, cover and cook for 1 hour in a preheated oven. Half an hour before the end of cooking time remove the cover to allow the ribs to crisp on top.

## TURKEY CROQUETTES
Serves 4

*8 oz (225 g) cold, cooked turkey*
*2 shallots, diced*
*1 tsp corn or soya oil*
*2 carrots, grated*
*6 oz (175 g) chestnuts, cooked and mashed with a little milk*
*2 eggs*
*4 oz (110 g) toasted breadcrumbs*

Finely dice the turkey. Fry the shallots in the oil in a small saucepan over low heat until they are transparent. Stir in the grated carrots and cook for a few minutes longer. Remove the pan from the heat and stir in the turkey. Beat in the mashed chestnuts and half the egg. Form the mixture into croquette shapes and dip them into the rest of the beaten egg. Roll the croquettes in the breadcrumbs. Fry or grill for about 20 minutes, turning to brown on both sides.

# STUFFED PEPPERS
Serves 4-6

*2 medium red peppers*
*2 medium yellow peppers*

*Stuffing:*
*4¹/₂ oz (120 g) chicken livers*
*1 oz (25 g) butter*
*1 tbsp oil*
*1 onion, finely chopped*
*1 clove garlic, finely chopped*
*1 tsp chopped fresh thyme, or a pinch of dried thyme*
*2 tbsp medium sweet sherry*
*4 oz (110 g) cream cheese*

Cut a lid from the stalk end of each pepper and remove all white pith and seeds. Trim the chicken livers, cutting away all stringy bits and flesh which is discoloured. Chop. Melt the oil and butter together and fry the onion and garlic until soft. Add the chicken livers and thyme and fry gently for about 5 minutes, stirring from time to time. Leave to cool. Add the sherry and then liquidise in a blender or food processor. Season to taste. Add the cream cheese and continue processing until all the ingredients are thoroughly blended. Spoon this mixture into the peppers and chill in the refrigerator. Just before serving cut into rings with a sharp knife and arrange on serving plates.

## SPICY CHICKEN WINGS
### Serves 9

*18 oz (500 g) carton soured cream*
*14 oz (400 g) blue cheese, crumbled*
*1 oz (25 g) parsley, chopped*
*2 oz (50 g) mayonnaise*
*1 tbsp milk*
*1 tbsp lemon juice*
*6 tbsp butter, melted*
*2 tbsp hot pepper sauce*
*18 chicken wings (about 3 lb/1.3 kg)*
*1 head of celery, cut into short sticks*

To make the blue cheese dip, mix the first six ingredients in a medium sized bowl and season to taste. Cover and refrigerate. Put the melted butter in a small saucepan and stir in the hot pepper sauce. Stir over low heat until well mixed. Arrange the chicken wings in a grill pan and sprinkle with salt. Brush with some of the hot pepper mixture and grill for about 10 minutes. Turn the chicken wings, brush with hot pepper mixture and grill for another 10 minutes until they are golden and tender. Make sure that they do not burn. Arrange the chicken wings on a platter, surrounded by the celery sticks. Serve the blue cheese dip on the side in a separate bowl.

## TERIYAKI CHICKEN
### Serves 4

*2 chicken legs or breasts, boned*
*2 tsp vegetable oil*
*4 fl oz (120 ml) dry white wine or saké*
*4 fl oz (120 ml) medium sweet sherry*
*2 fl oz (60 ml) soya sauce*
*1 tbsp sugar*
*2 cloves garlic, crushed*

Prick the chicken skin with a fork. Heat the oil and brown the chicken pieces. Remove from the pan. Meanwhile combine the remaining ingredients in a pan and bring to the boil. Pour into the chicken pan, stir and bring back to the boil. Put the chicken back in the pan and reduce the sauce over high heat, turning the chicken repeatedly. The chicken will soon be thickly coated and most of the sauce will be used up. Slice the chicken, skin side up, into 3/4 inch (2 cm) thick pieces. Garnish with lemon wedges and cucumber strips.

## HAM PARCELS
Serves 4

*4 slices of thinly cut ham*
*3 large hard-boiled eggs*
*2 tbsp mayonnaise*
*3 tbsp tuna, drained*
*2 tbsp parsley, chopped*
*freshly ground black pepper*

Cut each slice of ham into two long strips. Mash the hard-boiled eggs and the tuna together and bind with the mayonnaise. Stir in the chopped parsley and season with black pepper. Put a spoonful of the mixture at the end of one slice of ham and roll up. Secure with a cocktail stick until served if necessary. Serve on a bed of mixed lettuce.

## STUFFED BRIOCHES
Serves 4

*8 small brioches or 4 normal sized ones*
*2 smoked sausages, finely chopped*
*2 oz (50 g) ham, finely chopped*
*4 tbsp milk*
*4 tbsp cream*
*4 tbsp freshly grated Gruyère*
*1 tbsp cognac*

Cut the tops off the brioches and remove the crumb from the insides. Combine the crumb with the smoked sausages and ham. Add the milk, cream and Gruyère and cook over low heat, stirring, until a thick paste forms. Season. When ready to serve, reheat the mixture, stirring constantly. When it is very hot, remove from the heat and stir in the cognac. Fill the brioches with this mixture, replace the tops and heat in the oven for a few minutes until warmed through.

## LA CROUTE LANDAISE
### Makes 4

*4 thick slices of brioche*
*8 oz (225 g) button mushrooms, sliced*
*4 tbsp butter*
*4 tbsp double cream*
*salt and freshly ground black pepper*
*4 thin rounds mousse de foie gras.*
*¼ pt (150 ml) Béchamel Sauce*
*1 egg yolk*
*2 tbsp freshly grated Parmesan*

Simmer the sliced mushrooms in butter until soft. Puree them with the cream and season to taste with salt and freshly ground black pepper. Toast the brioche slices. Spread each slice thickly with mushroom puree and place on a baking sheet. Top each toast with a slice of foie gras and spoon hot Béchamel sauce, to which the egg yolk has been added, over each toast. Cover with freshly grated Parmesan and grill until golden.

## INDIAN CHICKEN
### Serves 4-6

*¼ pint (150 ml) mayonnaise*
*1 level tsp curry powder*
*8 oz (225 g) cooked chicken, chopped*
*8 oz (225 g) seedless grapes*
*1 red pepper, chopped*
*lettuce*

Beat the mayonnaise and curry powder together until blended. Stir in the chicken, grapes and red pepper and mix well. Arrange a couple of lettuce leaves on each plate and spoon some of the chicken mixture into the centre.

# CORONATION CHICKEN
Serves 6

*4 skinned and boned chicken breasts*
*1 onion, finely chopped*
*1 tbsp oil*
*1 clove garlic, crushed*
*2 tbsp mild curry paste*
*2 tbsp apricot jam*
*1/2 pint (300 ml) mayonnaise*
*1/2 pint (300 ml) natural yoghurt*
*2 red skinned eating apples*
*juice of 1/2 lemon*
*flaked almonds*

Stew the chicken breasts very gently in a little chicken stock until cooked right through. Leave to cool. When cold cut into bite-sized pieces. Sweat the onion and crushed garlic in the hot oil until softened but not browned. In a large bowl mix together the mayonnaise and yoghurt, then add the well drained onion and garlic and the curry paste. Stir well. Sieve the apricot jam and add it to the mixture. Cut the apples in half and remove the cores. Dice the flesh, retaining the red skin and toss with lemon juice. Mix into the sauce with the chunks of chicken. Sprinkle with toasted, flaked almonds before serving.

# HAM CORNETS
Serves 4

*3 oz (75 g) cream cheese*
*1 oz (25 g) mayonnaise*
*1 stick celery, chopped*
*2 spring onions, thinly sliced*
*1 oz (25 g) sultanas*
*2 oz (50 g) chopped walnuts*
*salt and pepper*
*4 thin slices ham*

Blend together the cream cheese and mayonnaise, thinning down with extra mayonnaise if necessary. Stir in all the other ingredients except the ham. Divide the mixture between the ham slices and roll up to form a cornet shape. Place on a serving dish.

# CHICKEN SATAY
Serves 4

*1 lb (450 g) chicken breast, cut into small cubes*
*2 tbsp dark soy sauce*
*3 tbsp lemon juice*
*1¹/₂ tsp ground ginger*
*4 oz (110 g) unsalted peanuts*
*2 tbsp oil*
*1 garlic clove, skinned and crushed*
*¹/₂ tsp ground coriander*
*¹/₄ tsp chilli powder*
*³/₄ pint (450 ml) coconut milk*
*1 tsp soft brown sugar*
*half cucumber, finely shredded*

Thread the chicken cubes onto 8 long satay sticks, or metal skewers. Mix together the soy sauce, lemon juice and 1 tsp of the ginger. Pour over the chicken and marinate for about 30 minutes, turning occasionally. Meanwhile finely chop or grind the peanuts. Heat the oil in a saucepan. Add the peanuts, garlic, coriander, chilli powder, remaining ginger and fry for 4-5 minutes until browned, stirring. Stir in the coconut milk and sugar. Bring to the boil and simmer for about 15 minutes until the sauce thickens. Season to taste. Grill the meat for about 6 minutes, until it is tender, turning occasionally. Serve the satay hot, with the cucumber, and the peanut sauce for dipping.

# FISH

## CRAB QUICHE
### Serves 6-8

*6 oz (175 g) shortcrust pastry*
*8 oz (225 g) crab meat*
*quarter cucumber, diced*
*3 eggs*
*³/₄ pint (450 ml) double cream*
*salt and freshly ground black pepper*

*Oven: 190°C/375°F/Gas Mk 5*

Prepare and bake blind an 8 inch (20 cm) flan case. Break up the crab meat with a fork. Place the eggs and cream in a bowl and beat together, then stir in the crab meat and add salt and pepper to taste, mixing until well blended. Spoon into the prepared flan case and bake in a preheated oven for 35-40 minutes until golden. Serve immediately.

## MEDITERRANEAN PEPPERS
### Serves 6

*3 large green peppers*
*6 oz (175 g) breadcrumbs*
*6 oz (175 g) cooked rice*
*2 oz (50 g) anchovy fillets*
*12 stoned black olives*
*2 tbsp tahini paste*
*1 egg*
*2 tbsp freshly chopped parsley*
*3 small tomatoes*

*Oven: 350°F/190°C/Gas Mk 4*

Preheat the oven. Wash the peppers. Slice in half lengthwise and remove seeds. Lightly oil an ovenproof dish and place the peppers in it. Mix together the breadcrumbs, rice, chopped anchovy fillets and olives, binding with the tahini and beaten egg. Stir in the parsley. Cut the tomatoes in half and place one half in the centre of each cut pepper, cut side uppermost. Pile the stuffing into the pepper around the tomato half. Pour ¹/₂ pint (300 ml) boiling water around the peppers and bake in the oven for about 40 minutes.

# TUNA AND APPLE JACKETS
Serves 4

*4 large baking potatoes*
*12 stuffed green olives*
*1 eating apple*
*7 oz (200 g) can tuna in oil*
*3 level tbsp natural strained Greek yoghurt*
*2 tbsp single cream*
*1 level tbsp creamed horseradish*
*lemon juice*

Scrub the potatoes and bake them in their jackets until tender.
Meanwhile slice the olives, roughly chop the apple and flake the tuna.
Mix together all the ingredients and add a dash of lemon juice. Season
to taste and spoon the mixture into the hot split potatoes.

# PISSALADIERE
Serves 4

*6 oz (175 g) rich shortcrust pastry*
*2 oz (50 g) tin anchovy fillets*
*small amount of milk*
*1 large green pepper, deseeded and cut in thin strips*
*1 large onion, skinned and sliced*
*butter and oil for frying*
*14 oz (400 g) tin tomatoes*
*1½ tsp sugar*
*½ tsp dried marjoram*
*½ tsp dried basil*
*grated Parmesan cheese*

*Oven: 190°C/375°F/Gas Mk 5*

Steep the anchovy fillets in milk for about 15 minutes, then drain.
Line an 8 inch (20 cm) flan tin with the pastry, prick the base with a
fork, cover with greaseproof paper and bake blind in a preheated oven
for about 10 minutes. Remove the paper and beans and bake for a further 5 minutes. Sauté the onion and pepper in the hot butter and oil
until soft and just golden. Add the tomatoes, sugar, herbs and season
well. Continue cooking gently for a further 10 minutes until the mixture becomes thick. Spread over the pastry base and criss-cross with
the anchovy fillets. Sprinkle with Parmesan cheese and bake in the
middle of the oven for 15-20 minutes. Leave to cool slightly, then
remove from the tin and leave to cool completely. Cut into slices.

# SMOKED SALMON FLAN
## Serves 6

*8 inch (20 cm) flan case, baked*
*6 wedges of lemon*

*Filling:*
*4 oz (110 g) smoked salmon pieces*
*freshly ground black pepper*
*2 eggs, beaten*
*4 tbsp milk*
*¼ pt (150 ml) single cream and fromage frais mixed together*
*1 tbsp chopped chives*

Heat the oven to 350°F/180°C/Gas mark 4. Place the flan case on an ovenproof serving dish. Put the salmon in the flan and season with pepper. Blend together all the remaining ingredients and pour over the salmon. Bake in the oven for about 30 minutes until the mixture is set and a pale golden brown colour. Serve with wedges of lemon.

# SALMON CREAM
## Serves 4

*½ oz (10 g) butter*
*1 level tbsp flour*
*¼ pt (150 ml) milk*
*8 oz (225 g) can red salmon*
*2 level tsp gelatine*
*1 tbsp tomato ketchup*
*2 tsp lemon juice*
*salt and pepper*
*¼ pt (150 ml) mayonnaise*
*cucumber slices to garnish*

Melt the butter in a small pan, stir in the flour and cook for a minute. Add the milk and bring to the boil, stirring, until the sauce thickens, then simmer for 2 minutes. Drain the juices from the can of salmon, place in a small bowl or cup with the gelatine and leave to soak for 3 minutes. Remove the white sauce from the heat and stir in the gelatine mixture until it has dissolved. Add the ketchup, lemon juice, salt and pepper and mix well. Remove any bones and black skin from the salmon and place the flesh in a food processor or blender with the sauce and mayonnaise. Liquidise until smooth. Divide the mixture between 4 serving dishes or ramekins and smooth the tops. Leave to set, then garnish with thin slices of cucumber.

# AVOCADO WITH PRAWNS
## Serves 4

*2 ripe avocados*
*juice of half lemon*
*½ pt (300 ml) cooked and shelled prawns*

*Dressing:*
*¼ pt (150 ml) double cream*
*2 tbsp wine vinegar*
*1 tsp mustard*
*1 tsp sugar*
*1 garlic clove, crushed with ½ tsp salt*
*paprika to garnish*

Make the dressing by whisking the cream and vinegar together in a bowl with a fork. Add the remaining ingredients and whisk until thoroughly combined. Stir the prawns into the dressing. Cut the avocados in half and remove the stones. Brush the flesh with lemon juice to keep the colour. Spoon the prawn mixture into the avocado halves and sprinkle the top of each with a little paprika. Serve with brown bread and butter.

# CRAB AND CELERY CANAPES
## Serves 4

*1 small crab or 1 medium-sized can of crabmeat*
*3 tbsp finely chopped celery*
*3 tbsp finely chopped parsley*
*few drops Tabasco sauce*

*Cream dressing:*
*3 tbsp mayonnaise*
*3 tbsp lightly whipped cream*
*good squeeze lemon juice*

*To serve:*
*fried bread croutons or lettuce leaves*
*yolks of 2 hard-boiled eggs*

Put the white crabmeat in a bowl and mix with the celery and parsley. Add a dash of Tabasco sauce to taste. Mix the cream dressing ingredients together, season and carefully mix into the crabmeat mixture. Serve piled onto fried bread croutons or, if preferred, lettuce leaves. Garnish with the dark crabmeat and sieved hard-boiled egg yolks.

# PRAWN VOL-AU-VENT FILLING
## Serves 4

*4 large (about 3 in/7.5 cm) vol-au-vent cases, cooked
(see recipe for Savoury Vol-au-vents on page 65)
1½ oz (35 g) butter
1 large onion, finely chopped
4 oz (110 g) button mushrooms, chopped
8 oz (225 g) shelled prawns
5 oz (150 ml) carton soured cream or fromage frais
salt and pepper*

Pre-heat the oven to 400°F/200°C/Gas mark 6. Fry the onion in melted butter over low heat until soft. Add the mushrooms and prawns to the pan and simmer for 2-3 minutes. Stir in the soured cream or fromage frais, heat gently and season to taste. Place in the vol-au-vent cases and heat in the oven for 10 minutes. Serve immediately.

# HERBED MUSSELS
## Serves 4-6

*4 lb (1.75 kg) mussels in their shells
3 cloves garlic, crushed
2 tsp grated lemon peel
3 tbsp parsley, chopped
1 sprig basil, chopped
2 sprigs thyme, chopped
1½ oz (35 g) fresh white breadcrumbs
5 tbsp olive oil*

Scrub the mussels thoroughly and then boil gently in about ½ pt (300 ml) boiling water for about 5 minutes, or until the shells have opened. Throw away any that have not opened, and drain the remainder. Break off and discard the empty half shell from each mussel and arrange the remaining halves in a large, shallow, flameproof dish. Mix the garlic, lemon rind, herbs and breadcrumbs together and sprinkle over the mussels. Gently spoon over the oil and place under a preheated moderate grill for 5-7 minutes until pale golden in colour. Serve immediately.

## SPICY PRAWNS WITH MELON
Serves 4

*1 ripe melon, well chilled*
*4 oz (110 g) shelled prawns*
*¼ pt (150 ml) soured cream*
*salt*
*pinch of curry powder*
*2 tsp mango chutney*
*small sprigs of mint to garnish*

Scoop out melon balls or small cubes from the melon. Mix with the prawns and place in four serving dishes. Season the soured cream with salt, a little curry powder and mango chutney and pour over the melon and prawns immediately prior to serving. Decorate with mint sprigs.

## SPICY MARINATED PLAICE
Serves 4

*12 oz (350 g) plaice fillet, skinned*
*2 tbsp soya sauce*
*3 tbsp olive oil*
*2 tsp wholegrain mustard*
*1 large clove garlic, crushed*
*2 red chillis, finely chopped*
*4 tbsp lemon juice*
*small piece fresh ginger root, crushed*
*salt and pepper to taste*
*6 oz (175 g) lettuce, finely shredded*
*2 spring onions, sliced*
*3 oz (75 g) button mushrooms, thinly sliced*
*fresh coriander to garnish*

Cut the plaice fillet into long, thin strips and place them in a shallow dish. Mix the soya sauce with the olive oil, mustard, garlic, chillis, lemon juice, ginger and salt and pepper. Spoon the marinade over the plaice and cover. Chill for 4 hours or preferably overnight. The fish will turn opaque. Mix together the lettuce, spring onions, and mushrooms and arrange as a border around 4 plates. Drain the marinated fish strips and place some in the middle of each plate. Trickle some of the marinade over the fish and the lettuce and garnish with coriander.

# BAKED AVOCADOS WITH TUNA
### Serves 4

*1 pt (600 ml) thick Béchamel Sauce*
*2 tbsp tomato puree*
*1 tbsp onion, grated*
*1 tbsp butter*
*14 oz (400 g) tuna, drained and flaked*
*2 ripe avocado pears*
*juice of 1 lemon*

*Oven: 350°F/180°C/Gas Mk 4*

After making the Béchamel sauce, add the tomato puree, onion and butter. Fold in the flaked tuna, season and heat gently. Do not boil. Halve the 2 avocados lengthwise, removing the stones. Sprinkle with lemon juice. Pile the tuna mix in the centres and place in an ovenproof dish. Put 1 inch (2.5 cm) of boiling water in the dish to surround the avocados and cover with foil. Bake in a low oven for about 20 minutes.

# TUNA DELIGHTS
### Serves 6

*8 fl oz (240 ml) soured cream or Greek yoghurt*
*2 tbsp mayonnaise*
*2 tsp snipped chives*
*2 tsp capers, chopped*
*1 tbsp onion, finely grated*
*dash Worcestershire sauce*
*2 tsp gelatine*
*2 tbsp warm water*
*1 x 7 oz (200 g) can tuna, drained and flaked*
*2 hard-boiled eggs, chopped*
*parsley sprigs to garnish*

Mix the soured cream or yoghurt with the mayonnaise, chives, capers and onion. Season to taste and add a dash of Worcestershire sauce. In a small bowl, melt the gelatine in the warm water, leave it until it is spongy and then put the bowl over a saucepan of hot water until the gelatine dissolves completely. Cool slightly and then stir into the soured cream mixture. Gently stir in the flaked tuna and chopped eggs and mix well. Pour into individual dishes and chill until set. Leave in the refrigerator until ready to serve. Garnish with a sprig of parsley on each and serve with thinly sliced brown bread and butter.

# AVOCADO WITH SALMON AND DILL
Serves 4

7½ oz (210 g) can red salmon, drained, skinned, boned and flaked
4 tbsp mayonnaise
1 tbsp fresh dill or ¼ tsp dried dill
juice of 1 lemon
salt and freshly ground black pepper
2 firm, ripe avocados
fresh dill and salad leaves

Mix the flaked salmon with the mayonnaise and dill. Add a little of the lemon juice to taste, then season with salt and plenty of black pepper. Halve, peel and slice the avocados. Brush with the remaining lemon juice to prevent the slices from turning brown. Spoon the salmon mixture onto serving plates with a fan of avocado slices. Garnish with sprigs of dill and some salad. Serve with fingers of wholemeal bread and butter.

# PRAWN AND CHIVE CROUSTADES
Serves 4

12 slices wholemeal bread
1½ oz (35 g) garlic and herb butter
½ oz (10 g) butter
½ oz (10 g) flour
¼ pt (150 ml) milk
1½ oz (35 g) Boursin cheese
6 oz (175 g) fresh peeled prawns
2 tbsp snipped chives

Flatten each slice of bread by rolling with a rolling pin. Cut out rounds of 4 in (10 cm) diameter with a fluted pastry cutter. Spread each round with garlic and herb butter. Press, buttered side down, into the hollows of a 12 section deep bun tray. Cook in a preheated oven (400°F/200°C/Gas Mk 6) for 12-15 minutes until golden brown. Leave in the bun trays to cool. Melt the butter in a saucepan, stir in the flour and cook gently for 1 minute. Gradually blend in the milk, stirring, until it boils and thickens. Stir in the Boursin cheese. Season if necessary. Leave to cool. Stir in the prawns and chives. Divide this mixture between the tartlet cases. Serve hot or cold with a side salad.

# HADDOCK CROWNS
Serves 4

*12 oz (350 g) haddock fillets*
*4 large tomatoes*
*2 tbsp mayonnaise*
*1 tbsp lemon juice*
*1 tbsp chopped mint*
*1 tbsp chopped parsley*
*2 tsp very finely chopped spring onions*
*lettuce*

Steam the fish and, when cooked, remove the skin and bones, and flake the flesh. Cool, then mix with mayonnaise, lemon juice, herbs and onion. Season to taste. Cut round the middle of the tomatoes with a sharp knife. Separate the halves, scoop out the seeds and discard. Remove as much of the flesh as possible, still keeping the skins firm. Chop the flesh and add to the fish mixture. Pile the fish mixture into the tomato cups and serve on a bed of lettuce.

# SCAMPI

FRIED SCAMPI: Coat the scampi with egg and breadcrumbs, fry in hot butter or deep fat for a few minutes only, until golden brown. Serve with lemon wedges and tartare sauce.

SCAMPI MEUNIÈRE: Do not coat the fish. Fry in hot butter for about 3 minutes. Remove from the pan with a slotted spoon and place on a serving dish. Add a little chopped parsley and a squeeze of lemon juice to the remaining butter and pour this over the scampi.

SCAMPI INDIENNE: Mix a little curry powder with the egg and breadcrumbs for coating and fry as above. Serve with lemon on a bed of boiled rice.

SCAMPI PROVENCALE: Fry a crushed clove of garlic and a very finely chopped onion in oil, together with two chopped, skinned and de-seeded tomatoes. Add the scampi and heat for a few minutes.

## SCALLOP KEBABS
Serves 4

*8 rashers bacon, derinded and halved*
*8 medium scallops, sliced*
*8-12 button mushrooms*
*1 oz (25 g) butter, melted*
*1 tbsp lemon juice*
*salt and freshly ground black pepper*
*lemon wedges to serve*

Roll up the bacon rashers. Thread scallop slices, bacon rolls and
mushrooms onto skewers. Brush with the butter and sprinkle with
the lemon juice and salt and pepper to taste. Cook under a hot grill
for about 5 minutes, turning several times. Serve with lemon wedges.

## TUNA AND SWEETCORN FILO LILIES
Serves 4

*1 oz (25g) butter*
*1 onion, finely chopped*
*6 oz (175 g) can sweetcorn*
*1 oz (25 g) plain flour*
*5 fl oz (150 ml) fish stock*
*6 oz (175 g) can evaporated milk*
*14 oz (400 g) tuna chunks, drained*
*3 tbsp freshly chopped chives*
*salt and black pepper*
*8 x 18 x 11 inch (46 cm x 28 cm) sheets of filo pastry*
*5 tbsp vegetable oil*

Pre-heat the oven to 190°C/375°F/Gas mark 5. Melt the butter in a
pan. Add the onion and fry for 3 minutes. Stir in the flour. Gradually
add the stock and evaporated milk, stirring continuously. Simmer for
2 minutes. Remove from the heat and stir in the tuna, sweetcorn and
chives. Season. Chill thoroughly. Cut the sheets of filo in half widthways. Brush four pieces with oil and stack keeping the corners irregular, like a water-lily. Pile a quarter of the mixture into the centre of
the top sheet. Gather the pastry around the filling. Pinch to position,
leaving the corners sticking up. Transfer to an oiled baking sheet.
Brush with oil. Repeat to make four lilies. Bake for 20-25 minutes or
until golden. Serve with crisp salad.

## TUNA STUFFED AVOCADO
Serves 6

*3 avocados*
*juice of 1 small lemon*
*4 tbsp mayonnaise*
*7 oz (200 g) can tuna chunks, well drained*
*salt and pepper*
*3½ oz (85 g) can sweetcorn, well drained*

Mix together the mayonnaise, tuna, sweetcorn and seasoning. Halve the avocado pears and remove the stones. Carefully scoop out the flesh and blend this with the tuna mixture. Pile the mixture back into the avocado skins and squeeze lemon juice on top. Serve as soon as possible after preparing with thinly sliced brown bread and butter.

## CHILLI FISH BALLS
Serves 6

*1 lb (450 g) white fish fillets*
*¼ pt (150 ml) milk*
*6 black peppercorns*
*sprig of coriander*
*1 lb (450 g) potatoes, peeled*
*1 large onion, finely grated*
*2 oz (50 g) fresh white breadcrumbs*
*1 red pepper, seeded and finely diced*
*2 tbsp fresh, chopped coriander*
*¼ tsp chilli powder*
*juice of half lemon*
*1 egg, lightly beaten*
*oil for deep-frying*
*salad to serve*

Place the fish in a large pan with the milk, peppercorns and coriander sprig. Cook gently for 5 minutes until the fish just flakes. Drain the fish and flake into a bowl, discarding the skin and any bones. In a separate bowl, finely grate the potatoes. Drain off any juices and mix the potatoes into the fish. Add the onion to the fish mixture with the breadcrumbs, pepper, coriander, chilli powder and seasoning. Bind with the lemon juice and egg. Shape into 24 small balls. Heat the oil to 180°C/350°F or until a piece of bread dropped into the hot oil turns golden brown within 30 seconds. Deep-fry the fish balls in batches of 6 for 4-5 minutes. Drain on kitchen paper. Place the fish balls on individual plates and serve with a side salad.

## PRAWN COCKTAIL
Serves 4-6

*6 oz (175 g) shelled prawns*
*small lettuce*
*¼ cucumber, chopped finely*

*Sauce:*
*¼ pt (150 ml) mayonnaise*
*1 tsp tomato puree*
*pinch caster sugar*
*1 tbsp lemon juice*
*2 tbsp double cream*
*salt and pepper*

*To serve:*
*sliced lemon*
*brown bread and butter*

Finely shred the lettuce and mix with the chopped cucumber. Place in 4-6 individual serving glasses. Make the sauce by mixing together all the ingredients, check the seasoning and gently stir in prawns. Spoon over the lettuce and cucumber base. Garnish with slices of fresh lemon and serve with small slices of brown bread and butter.

## PUREE OF TUNA FISH
Serves 2

*2 oz (50 g) tuna fish*
*2 hard-boiled egg yolks*
*2 oz (50 g) butter*
*salt and freshly ground black pepper*
*1 sprig parsley*
*1 tsp chervil*

Puree the tuna and the butter together in a blender or food processor. Season well with pepper and a little salt. Pass the egg yolks through a sieve, and mix with the finely chopped parsley and chervil. This puree can be used as a starter by filling the hard boiled whites of egg, or hollowed-out cherry tomatoes, or tinned artichoke hearts as part of hors-d'oeuvre. Alternatively, it makes a good canapé spread.

# FISH IN SOUR CREAM
Serves 6

*6 soused herrings*
*6 spring onions, finely chopped*
*2 small eating apples*
*3 oz (75 g) pickled beetroot*
*salt and freshly ground black pepper*
*8 fl oz (240 ml) soured cream*
*8 fl oz (240 ml) mayonnaise*
*(or half mayonnaise, half natural yoghurt)*

*To serve:*
*watercress sprigs to garnish*
*brown bread and butter*

If possible prepare the soused herrings flat instead of rolled. Place the fish on a serving dish. Peel, core and dice the apples and mix with the finely chopped onions. Dice the beetroot and mix in. Lightly whisk the cream and combine with the mayonnaise and onion mixture. Season well. Spoon the dressing carefully over the fish. Garnish with the watercress sprigs and serve with finely sliced brown bread and butter.

# POTTED SHRIMPS

*8 oz (225 g) peeled frozen prawns*
*8 oz (225 g) butter (unsalted is preferable)*
*³/₄ tsp grated nutmeg*
*ground black pepper*
*pinch of cayenne pepper*

Defrost the prawns. Melt the butter and add the nutmeg, pepper and cayenne. Stir in the prawns and cook gently for about 5 minutes, stirring occasionally. Adjust seasoning if required. Pour into ramekins and chill.

# FISH SURPRISE
Serves 4

*4 flat fish fillets, skinned*

*Filling:*
*2 oz (50 g) white breadcrumbs*
*2 tbsp finely chopped gherkins*
*1 tbsp finely chopped capers*
*2 tbsp finely chopped spring onions*
*1 tbsp lemon juice*
*1 egg, beaten*

*Sauce:*
*3 tbsp white wine*
*1 oz (25 g) butter*
*2 tbsp single cream*

*Oven: 400°F/200°C/Gas Mk 6*

Slice fillets in half lengthwise. Combine all the filling ingredients, place a spoonful of the mixture on each fillet half and roll up from the head to the tail. Butter an ovenproof dish and arrange the rolled fillets in the dish, packing closely together to keep their shape. If the dish is too large use cocktail sticks through each roll to keep the fillets in shape, but remember to remove them before serving. Pour the wine over and dot the top of each fillet with a knob of butter. Cover the dish with foil and bake for 15 minutes or until the fish is opaque. Put the cooked fillets in a serving dish and keep warm. Pour the cooking juices into a saucepan and bring to the boil. Reduce the juices by fast boiling, add the cream and season to taste. Pour the sauce over the fish.

# SMOKED TROUT FINGERS
Serves 4

*4 smoked trout fillets*
*4-6 tbsp double cream*
*2 tbsp olive oil*
*juice of ½ lemon*
*salt and freshly ground black pepper*
*sliced white bread*
*softened butter*
*parsley, chopped*

Remove all the skin and bones from the trout and liquidise or process to a smooth paste with the cream and olive oil. Add the lemon juice to taste, together with the salt and black pepper. Toast white bread and cut it into fingers. Spread with the softened butter and pile the smoked trout paste on top. Sprinkle with chopped parsley.

# PORTUGUESE SARDINES

*1 x 7½ oz (210 g) can sardines in oil*
*3 tbsp finely chopped onions*
*2 tbsp chopped pimientos*
*4 slices crisp bacon, crumbled*
*1 tbsp finely chopped mushrooms*
*1 tbsp finely chopped celery*
*1 tbsp finely chopped almonds*
*freshly ground black pepper*
*¼ tsp paprika*

*Sauce:*
*2 tbsp Worcestershire sauce*
*4 oz (110 g) mayonnaise*
*2 oz (50 g) ketchup*
*2 tbsp lemon juice*
*1 tsp mustard*

Mash the undrained sardines and then mix in the rest of the ingredients. Pile onto individual plates or place in ramekins. Chill in the refrigerator. For the sauce, mix together the mayonnaise, ketchup, Worcestershire sauce, lemon juice and mustard and turn into a small bowl. Garnish the sardines with slices of tomato and cucumber. Serve with toast squares or fingers. The sardine mix should be spread on the toast and the dressing spooned over.

## PRAWN AND MUSHROOM CREAM
Serves 4

*6 oz (175 g) peeled prawns*
*4 oz (110 g) mushrooms*
*2 bunches watercress*

*Dressing:*
*1 clove garlic crushed*
*5 oz (150 g) natural yoghurt*
*2 tbsp mayonnaise*
*1 tbsp lemon juice*
*2 tbsp tomato ketchup*
*2 spring onions*

Wipe the mushrooms, slice finely and mix with the peeled prawns in a bowl. Put the well crushed garlic clove into a mixing bowl together with the natural yoghurt, mayonnaise, lemon juice and tomato ketchup. Season well and beat all the ingredients together until they are well mixed. Mix in the prawns and mushrooms. Wash, trim and pat dry the watercress and divide between 4 plates. Put a pile of prawn and mushroom cream on the watercress and sprinkle over the finely chopped spring onions.

## SMOKED FISH CREAM
Serves 6

*8 oz (225 g) smoked haddock*
*1/2 pt (300 ml) milk*
*1 oz (25 g) butter*
*1 oz (25 g) flour*
*freshly ground black pepper*
*1/4 pt (150 ml) made-up aspic jelly*
*3 tbsp double cream*

Poach the haddock gently in milk for about 10 minutes, or until tender. Remove the skin and bones, if any, and flake the fish finely. Melt the butter, stir in the flour and cook the roux for 1 minute. Strain in the milk the haddock was poached in, stirring continuously. Bring to the boil and simmer for 2-3 minutes until thickened, stirring all the time. Season well with pepper. Pound the fish and gradually work in the sauce, stir in the melted aspic jelly and the cream. Pour into 6 ramekins or 1 large mould if preferred. Refrigerate until set and keep refrigerated until ready to use. Garnish with gherkins cut into fan shapes and serve with toast fingers or brown bread and butter.

# TUNA AND CORN MOULDS
## Serves 4

*1 level tbsp powdered gelatine*
*6 fl oz (180 ml) vegetable stock*
*1 x 7 oz (200 g) can sweetcorn, drained*
*1 x 7 oz (200 g) can tuna, drained and flaked*
*salt and freshly ground black pepper*
*sprigs of watercress or mustard and cress to garnish*

Put the gelatine and 3 tbsp vegetable juice into a cup. Stand in a pan of hot water and stir until melted. Meanwhile wet the inside of 4 dariole moulds. Divide half the corn between each container, then cover with half the flaked tuna, then repeat these layers until all the mixture is used up. Stir the gelatine into the remaining vegetable juice. Season to taste and pour into the moulds, filling them almost to the top. Chill to set. When the moulds are set, dip briefly into hot water, loosen the edges and tip out onto individual plates. Garnish with watercress or mustard and cress.

# CHEESE, SHRIMP AND MUSHROOM RAMEKINS
## Serves 4

*2 oz (50 g) mushrooms, wiped and sliced*
*1½ oz (35 g) butter*
*¼ oz (5 g) flour*
*¼ pt (150 ml) milk*
*3 eggs, hard-boiled*
*2 oz (50 g) Cheddar cheese, grated*
*4 oz (110 g) shrimps, peeled*
*salt and freshly ground pepper*

Fry the mushrooms in ½ oz (10 g) of the butter until soft. Melt ¼ oz (5 g) butter for the sauce in a small pan, stir in the flour and cook gently for 1 minute, stirring. Remove the pan from the heat and gradually stir in the milk. Bring to the boil slowly and continue to cook, stirring, until the sauce thickens. Roughly chop the eggs and add to the sauce with 1 oz (25 g) cheese, the shrimps and fried mushrooms. Season. Stir in the remaining butter and reheat without boiling. Pour into 4 buttered ramekin dishes. Sprinkle the remaining grated cheese on top and brown under a hot grill. Serve at once.

# FISH CREAMS
Serves 4

*8 oz (225 g) haddock*
*whites of 2 small eggs*
*¼ pt (150 ml) cream*
*2-3 egg yolks*
*3 fl oz (90 ml) cream*
*4 oz (110 g) mushrooms, sliced*

*Sauce:*
*¾ oz (15 g) butter*
*½ oz (10 g) flour*
*7 fl oz (200 ml) fish stock*
*squeeze of lemon juice*

Skin, bone and mince the fish and put into a bowl. Whisk the egg whites gently and beat into the fish a little at a time. Blend or pass through a sieve and return to the basin. Beat in the cream slowly, adding seasoning. Put the mixture into buttered cutlet or quenelle moulds, pressing down firmly with a knife. Poach or steam in a shallow bain marie two-thirds full of boiling salted water for 7-10 minutes. For the sauce melt the butter and stir in the flour, blending well. Off the heat pour in the warmed fish stock, return to the heat and stir until boiling. Add a squeeze of lemon juice and simmer for a few minutes. Meanwhile cook the sliced mushrooms gently with a nut of butter, 1 tsp of lemon juice and a dessertspoon of water. Cream the egg yolks in a bowl, season well with salt and pepper and mix in the cream. Stir into the sauce on a very low heat, add the sliced mushrooms and serve immediately, poured over the fish creams.

# PRAWNS IN GARLIC
Serves 4-6

*1 oz (25 g) butter*
*2 tbsp oil*
*2 cloves garlic, crushed*
*8 oz (225 g) long-grain rice*
*2 tbsp chopped parsley*
*10 oz peeled prawns*
*juice of ½ lemon*

Heat the butter and oil together in a pan and fry the garlic for 2 minutes. Add the prawns and cook quickly for 2 minutes. Stir in the parsley and lemon juice and serve immediately, with hot crusty bread.

## SMOKED SALMON AND TAMARA TIMBALES
### Serves 4

*6 oz (175 g) smoked salmon, thinly sliced*
*6 oz (175 g) taramasalata*
*6 oz (175 g) full fat soft cheese*
*dash of Tabasco sauce*
*juice of 1/2 lemon*
*shake of cayenne pepper*
*oil, for greasing*
*4 twists lemon to garnish*

Oil 4 ramekin dishes. Line the dishes with smoked salmon and chop any that is left over. Mix together the taramasalata, soft cheese, Tabasco sauce, lemon juice and cayenne pepper. Add any remaining chopped salmon. Divide this mixture between the 4 dishes. Level the tops and chill for 2-3 hours. Carefully turn out of the dishes and garnish with twists of lemon.

## FISH CROQUETTES
### Serves 4

*1 lb (450 g) white fish*
*1 oz (25 g) butter*
*1 tbsp flour*
*1 1/2 pt (900 ml) milk*
*4 oz (110 g) white breadcrumbs*
*salt, pepper, nutmeg*
*dash of curry powder*
*egg and breadcrumbs for coating*
*oil for deep-frying*

Poach the fish gently in fish stock or court bouillon. Cool, remove all the skin and bones and flake finely. Melt the butter, add the flour, stirring, and cook gently for about 3 minutes. Bring the milk to the boil in another pan and pour into the roux (flour and butter mix) whisking until the sauce thickens. Cook gently for another 3 minutes. Add the fish and breadcrumbs, season well and add the seasoning and curry powder. Spread the mixture on a plate to cool. Roll into small croquettes between floured hands, coat with beaten egg and roll in breadcrumbs. Heat the oil and, when it is hot enough, deep-fry the croquettes until they are golden brown. Drain on kitchen paper and serve hot.

# HADDOCK AND SHRIMP GRATIN
Serves 6

*1 lb (450 g) haddock fillet, skinned*
*1 oz (25 g) butter*
*1 medium onion, finely chopped*
*3 level tbsp flour*
*½ pt (300 ml) milk*
*3 tbsp dry white wine*
*6½ oz (185 g) can shrimps*
*3 oz (75 g) Cheddar cheese, grated*
*salt and freshly ground pepper*

*Oven: 375°F/190°C/Gas Mk 5*

Cut the haddock fillet into twelve small strips. Fold strips in half and place two in each of six individual ramekin or gratin dishes. Melt the butter in a saucepan and sauté the finely chopped onion until softened. Stir in the flour and cook gently for 1 minute. Remove the pan from the heat and gradually stir in the milk, wine and strained juices from the shrimps. Bring to the boil slowly and continue to cook, stirring, until the sauce thickens. Remove the pan from the heat and add the shrimps and 2 oz (50 g) grated cheese to the sauce. Season. Spoon a little into each ramekin. Scatter the remaining cheese on top. Cook in the oven for 30 minutes. Serve immediately.

# GOUJONS OF TROUT WITH HAZELNUTS
Serves 4

*2 trout, skinned and filleted*
*2 oz (50 g) hazelnuts, skinned and chopped*
*4 oz (110 g) fresh white breadcrumbs*
*1 oz (25 g) seasoned flour*
*2 eggs, beaten*
*oil, for deep frying*
*lemon wedges*

Cut the trout into strips diagonally. Mix together the hazelnuts and breadcrumbs in a bowl. Coat the fish with seasoned flour, dip in the egg, then roll in the breadcrumb mixture. Chill for about 30 minutes. Deep fry in the hot oil in 2 batches for 5 minutes each batch. Drain well on kitchen paper, keeping the first batch hot while the other batch is cooking. Divide between 4 plates and serve with lemon wedges.

# INDIVIDUAL SEAFOOD PIZZAS
## Serves 8

*½ tsp dried yeast*
*½ tsp caster sugar*
*6 oz (175 g) strong white plain flour*
*2 oz (50 g) butter*
*1 egg, beaten*
*little milk to mix*

*Topping:*
*2½ oz (60 g) tomato puree*
*8 oz (225 g) tomatoes*
*3½ oz (85 g) can tuna, drained*
*2 oz (50 g) prawns*
*½ tsp dried oregano*
*½ tsp dried basil*
*1 tbsp olive oil*
*2 oz (50 g) cheese, grated*
*few black olives (optional)*
*1¾ oz (40 g) can anchovy fillets (optional)*

*Oven: 400°F/200°C/Gas Mk 6*

Dissolve the yeast and sugar in a little warm water. Sift the flour and a pinch of salt into a bowl and rub in the butter until the mixture resembles fine breadcrumbs. Mix in the dissolved yeast, beaten egg and as much milk as is required to make a firm but not sticky dough. Knead for 5-10 minutes until the dough is smooth. Place in a buttered bowl, cover with a cloth and leave to rise in a warm place until doubled in size - about 1½ hours. Knead again, divide into 8 pieces and roll into circles about 4 in (10 cm) in diameter. Place on oiled baking sheets and spread with tomato puree. Slice the skinned tomatoes and arrange on top. Cover with the tuna and prawns, sprinkle with the herbs and a little olive oil. Bake in the oven for 10 minutes Top with the cheese, and the olives and anchovies if using. Return to the oven for 5 minutes. Serve hot.

## SCALLOPS NANTUA
### Serves 6

*8 oz (225 g) freshwater crayfish or prawns in their shells*
*1 slice onion, 3 slices carrot, 1 bay leaf*
*12 scallops*
*1 oz (25 g) butter*
*1 oz (25 g) flour*
*2 tbsp double cream*
*2 oz (50 g) butter*
*3 oz (75 g) breadcrumbs*

Place the crayfish or prawns in a saucepan and pour in ¾ pt (450 ml) water. Add the onion, carrot and bay leaf. Bring to the boil, and continue boiling rapidly until the liquid has reduced by approximately one third. Reduce the heat and add the scallops. Simmer gently for 10 minutes. If the scallops are cooked too quickly they tend to become rubbery in texture. Strain off the liquid and reserve. Separate the scallops and cut each one into 4. Set aside. Peel the crayfish or prawns and pass through a liquidiser or food processor together with ½ pt (300 ml) of the fish liquor. Melt the butter in a saucepan, add the flour and cook the roux for 2-3 minutes. Remove from the heat and gently stir in the fish puree. Return to the heat and slowly bring to the boil. Stir in the cream and scallops, and season. Divide the mixture between 6 deep scallop shells or individual ovenproof dishes. Melt the butter and stir in the breadcrumbs. Sprinkle over the top of each dish and brown under the grill. Serve with lemon slices.

## SEAFOOD COCKTAIL
### Serves 4

*12 oz (350 g) shelled and prepared shellfish (prawns, crab, lobster, etc.)*
*¼ pint (150 ml) mayonnaise*
*1 tbsp tomato puree*
*2 tbsp thick cream*
*2 tsp lemon juice*
*2 tsp Worcestershire sauce*
*shredded lettuce, slices of cucumber and lemon to serve.*

Flake or cut the fish into bite-sized pieces and place in a mixing bowl. Blend remaining ingredients together, fold into the fish mixture, coating well, and season. Put shredded lettuce in the bottom of 4 glass dishes, pile the fish mixture on top and garnish with cucumber and lemon slices. Serve with brown bread and butter.

# MONKFISH AURORE
Serves 4

*1 lb (450 g) monkfish*
*¼ pt (150 ml) mayonnaise*
*3 tbsp double or whipping cream, whipped*
*1 tbsp lemon juice*
*1 tsp tomato puree*
*1 tbsp chopped capers*
*1 tbsp chopped gherkins*
*4 gherkins fans to garnish*
*4 lemon slices to garnish*

Cut the monkfish into 1 in (2.5 cm) cubes, put in a pan of lightly salted water, bring to the boil and simmer for 10 minutes. Remove from the heat and leave to cool in the liquid. In a bowl mix together the mayonnaise, cream, lemon juice, tomato puree, capers and gherkins. Season. Strain the cooled fish and add to the mayonnaise mixture. Divide between 4 plates and garnish with gherkins and lemon slices.

# SOUSED HERRINGS
Serves 6

*6 small herrings*
*1 onion, sliced*
*2 bay leaves*
*1 clove*
*3 allspice berries or peppercorns*
*1 tsp salt*
*4 fl oz (120 ml) white wine vinegar*

Clean and scale the fish and remove the fish heads. Place the fish on a work surface, cut off the fillets and remove any bones. Place slices of onion in the centre of each fillet and roll up, skin side out, from head to tail. Fix with a cocktail stick. Place the rolled herrings in a heavy, ovenproof casserole with the bay leaves, clove, allspice or peppercorns and salt. Pour over the vinegar and just cover with water. Cover and cook over low heat for 1-1½ hours or until the fish flakes easily when tested with a fork. Transfer the fish to a serving dish deep enough for the fish to be covered with the liquid. Strain over sufficient cooking liquid to cover the fish. Cool, then chill in the refrigerator where the liquor will set into a soft jelly. Serve with cucumber salad. This dish will keep for up to 2 weeks in the refrigerator.

## PRAWN AND MUSHROOM FILO LILIES
Serves 4

*1 oz (25 g) butter*
*1 onion, finely chopped*
*2 oz (50 g) button mushrooms, chopped*
*1 oz (25 g) plain flour*
*5 fl oz (150 ml) fish stock*
*6 oz (175 g) can evaporated milk*
*8 oz (225 g) shelled prawns*
*3 tbsp freshly chopped chives*
*8 x 18 x 11 in (46 x 28 cm) sheets of filo pastry*
*5 tbsp vegetable oil*
*crisp salad to serve*

Pre-heat the oven to 190°C/375°F/Gas mark 5. Melt the butter in a pan. Add the onion and mushrooms and fry for 3 minutes. Stir in the flour. Gradually add the stock and evaporated milk, stirring continuously. Simmer for 2 minutes. Remove from the heat and stir in the prawns and chives. Season. Chill thoroughly. Cut the sheets of filo in half widthways. Brush four pieces with oil and stack, keeping the corners irregular, like a water-lily. Pile a quarter of the mixture into the centre of the top sheet. Gather the pastry around the filling. Pinch to position, leaving the corners sticking out like a flower. Transfer to an oiled baking sheet. Brush with oil. Repeat to make four lilies. Bake for 20-25 minutes until golden. Serve with crisp salad.

## AVOCADO SURPRISE
Serves 4

*2 avocados*
*7 oz (200 g) can tuna fish, drained*
*4 oz (110 g) cream cheese*
*1 tbsp lemon juice*
*4 black olives*
*parsley, chopped*

Cut the avocados in half and remove the stones. Scoop out most of the flesh of the avocado halves, leaving just enough on the skins to retain their shape. Place the flesh in a bowl, and add the tuna fish, cream cheese and lemon juice and beat well. Season to taste. If the mixture is too firm, add a little more lemon juice. Pile into the avocado skins, garnish with a stoned black olive and sprinkle with the parsley.

# PRAWN TARTLETS
Makes 20 tartlets

2 oz (50 g) butter
2 oz (50 g) plain flour
1 pt (600 ml) milk
few drops anchovy essence
¹/₂-1 tbsp tomato paste
1 lb (450 g) peeled prawns
13 oz (375 g) shortcrust pastry
20 peeled prawns to garnish
20 sprigs parsley to garnish
paprika to garnish

*Oven: 190°C/375°F/Gas mark 5*

Make pastry, or use thawed frozen shortcrust pastry. Roll out and cut 20 circles measuring 3 inches (7.5 cm) in diameter. Place the circles in tartlet tins, prick the bases and bake blind in the oven for about 15 minutes until a light golden colour. Cool on a wire tray.
Meanwhile stir the flour into the melted butter to make a roux and cook gently for 2-3 minutes, stirring all the time. Gradually blend in the milk, bringing gently to simmering point and simmer for 5 minutes. Add the anchovy essence and tomato paste to taste, pour into a large bowl, cover and leave to cool. When the sauce is cold, stir in the prawns and season to taste. Fill the tartlets with this mixture, garnish with prawns, and parsley sprigs and dust with paprika pepper

# CHEESE AND SHRIMP SOUFFLES
Serves 4

2 large eggs
¹/₄ pt (150 ml) single cream
1 tsp English mustard
pinch of cayenne pepper
3 oz (75 g) peeled shrimps
4 oz (110 g) matured Cheddar cheese, finely grated
1 tbsp freshly grated Parmesan cheese

Beat together the eggs, cream, mustard and cayenne and season to taste. Stir in the shrimps and cheeses. Lightly grease four individual soufflé dishes and pour in the mixture. Bake in a preheated oven (200°C/400°F/Gas Mark 6) for 20-25 minutes, until well risen and golden brown. Serve immediately.

## SHELLFISH CAPRICE
Serves 4-6

*1 lb (450 g) shelled and prepared shellfish (prawns, crab, lobster, etc.)*
*½ pint (300 ml) mayonnaise.*
*1 tbsp tomato puree*
*3 tbsp thick cream*
*3 tsp lemon juice*
*2 tsp Worcestershire sauce*
*2 dessert apples (red-skinned)*
*2 sticks celery*
*¼ cucumber*
*salt and pepper*

Wash and core the apples, leaving peel on. Slice half an apple thinly and dice the remainder. Sprinkle with lemon juice. Chop the celery finely, cut a few slices of cucumber and dice the remainder. Combine the diced apple, celery and cucumber with the fish. To make the sauce, blend the remaining ingredients together and fold into the fish mixture, coating well. Place in 4-6 individual dishes and garnish with slices of apple and cucumber and a sprig of parsley. Serve with brown bread and butter.

## MARINATED KIPPER FILLETS
Serves 6

*1 lb (450 g) frozen kipper fillets, thawed*
*6 tbsp olive oil*
*3 tbsp lemon juice*
*1 tbsp chopped parsley*
*1 tbsp chopped chives*
*pepper*

*Garnish:*
*onion rings*
*lemon slices*
*parsley sprigs*

Remove the skin and any bones from the kippers. Cut into thin slivers and place in a bowl. Mix together the oil, lemon juice and herbs and add pepper to taste. Pour over the kippers and toss well to coat the fish thoroughly. Cover and chill for 2-3 hours. Transfer to a serving dish and garnish with onion rings, lemon slices and parsley sprigs. Serve with brown bread and butter.

# TUNA FLAN
Serves 6

*8 inch (20 cm) flan case, baked*
*7 oz (200 g) can tuna chunks*
*freshly ground black pepper*
*2 eggs, beaten*
*4 tbsp milk*
*¼ pt (150 ml) single cream and fromage frais mixed together*
*1 tbsp chopped chives*

Heat the oven to 350°F/180°C/Gas mark 4. Place the flan case on an ovenproof serving dish. Put the tuna in the flan and season. Blend together all the remaining ingredients and pour over the tuna. Bake for about 30 minutes until the filling is set and a pale golden brown.

# SMOKED HADDOCK ROULADE
Serves 6

*2 oz (50 g) plain flour*
*4 large eggs, separated*
*2 tbsp water*
*4 oz (110 g) Cheddar cheese, grated*
*4 tbsp freshly grated Parmesan cheese*

*Filling:*
*1 oz (25 g) butter*
*1 oz (25 g) plain flour*
*⅓ pt (200 ml) milk*
*8 oz (225 g) smoked haddock fillets, cooked, skinned and flaked*
*1 hard-boiled egg, chopped*
*1 tbsp chopped parsley*

Sift the flour into a bowl and beat in the egg yolks and water until smooth. Stir in the Cheddar cheese and half the Parmesan and season. Whisk the egg whites until stiff and carefully fold in. Spread evenly in a lined and greased 12 x 8 inch (30 x 20 cm) Swiss roll tin and bake in a preheated oven at 200°C/400°F/Gas Mark 6 for 15 minutes, until well risen and golden brown. Meanwhile, melt the butter in a pan, add the flour and cook for 1 minute, stirring. Gradually stir in the milk and cook, stirring, for 1 minute. Season. Fold in the haddock, chopped egg and parsley. Sprinkle the remaining Parmesan over a large piece of greaseproof paper. Turn out the roulade onto this paper, removing the lining paper. Spread the filling over the surface and carefully roll up like a Swiss roll. Serve immediately.

# WHITEBAIT
### Serves 4

*1½ lb (675 g) whitebait*
*3 oz (75 g) seasoned flour*
*oil for deep frying*
*lemon wedges*
*parsley*

Wash and drain the whitebait. Toss the whitebait in the flour. Heat the oil to 375°F/190°C in a large deep-fryer or pan. Place the white-bait in the basket a few at a time and deep-fry each batch for about 2 minutes until crisp and cooked through. Lift out and drain on kitchen paper. Pile onto a warm serving dish and garnish with lemon wedges and sprigs of parsley. Serve with thinly sliced brown bread and butter.

# PRAWN PILAU
### Serves 6

*2 oz (50 g) butter*
*1 small onion, finely chopped*
*1 clove garlic, crushed*
*8 oz (225 g) long-grain rice*
*⅓ pt (200 ml) dry white wine*
*2-3 strands of saffron*
*3 oz (75 g) mushrooms, sliced*
*1 pt (600 ml) fish or chicken stock*
*4 tomatoes, skinned, seeded and chopped*
*1 tbsp chopped basil*
*8 oz (225 g) peeled prawns*

Gently cook the onion and garlic in melted butter for about 5 min-utes. Add the rice, wine and saffron and bring to the boil, stirring. Cook until most of the wine has evaporated, stirring constantly. Stir in ⅔ of the stock and season. Bring to the boil, cover and simmer for 5 minutes. Add the sliced mushrooms and continue simmering for another 10 minutes or until the rice is just tender, stirring occasional-ly. If necessary, add more stock to keep the rice moist. Stir in the tomatoes, basil and prawns and cook for 2 minutes. Serve with Parmesan cheese.

# CREAMED SOLE IN MUSHROOM SAUCE
Serves 6

*3 large lemon sole, filleted*
*freshly ground black pepper*
*knob of butter*
*10½ oz (310 g) can condensed mushroom soup*
*2 tbsp sherry*
*1 tbsp chopped parsley*
*a few bunches of white grapes to garnish*

Heat the oven to 350 °C/180°C/Gas mark 4. Butter a shallow 2 pint (1.1 ltr) ovenproof dish. Sprinkle the fish with ground black pepper and roll up, skin side inwards. Place the fillets standing upright in the dish. Put the undiluted soup into a small bowl and blend in the sherry and parsley, then pour over the fish. Cover with a lid or foil and bake in the oven for 25 minutes or until the fillets look white and the flesh flakes easily. Remove the lid and serve the dish garnished with small bunches of grapes.

# SMOKED SALMON OR TROUT

Arrange one or two slices of smoked salmon per person on serving plates with a good wedge of lemon. Garnish with lettuce leaves. Serve with cayenne or paprika and thin brown bread and butter. Smoked trout is served with horseradish cream. Allow one fillet per person.

# TROUT FILLETS WITH CUCUMBER AND DILL
Serves 4

*4 smoked trout fillets*
*1 cucumber*
*1 tbsp salad oil*
*2 tbsp hot water*
*2 tbsp wine vinegar*
*2 tbsp caster sugar*
*chopped fresh dill*

Put the trout fillets on one side of a serving plate. Peel the cucumber, cut into very thin slices and lay in a shallow dish. Blend the oil, water, vinegar and sugar together, in a blender if possible, season and pour over the cucumber. Refrigerate. When ready to serve, spoon the cucumber onto the serving plate alongside the trout fillets and sprinkle with chopped dill.

# MUSSELS IN CURRY SAUCE
Serves 4-6

*4 lb (1.75 kg) mussels in their shells*
*1 oz (25 g) butter*
*1 small onion, finely chopped*
*1 tsp curry powder*
*1 tsp tomato puree*
*4 tbsp dry white wine*
*2 tbsp apricot jam, sieved*
*1/4 pt (150 ml) double cream*
*1/4 pt (150 ml) mayonnaise*
*juice of half lemon*
*12 oz (350 g) cooked long-grain rice, cooled*

Scrub the mussels clean, then cook in a pan containing 1/2 pt (300 ml) boiling water for about 5 minutes, until the shells have opened. Discard any that do not open. Drain. Reserve a few mussels for garnish and remove the rest from their shells. Melt the butter in a pan, add the onion and sauté for 2-3 minutes. Stir in the curry powder and fry for a few minutes, then stir in the tomato puree, wine, apricot jam, and season to taste. Leave to cool. Lightly whip the cream, then fold into the sauce with the mayonnaise and lemon juice. Cover and chill for 2-3 hours, then fold in the shelled mussels. Arrange the rice on individual serving dishes and spoon the mussel mixture into the centre

# PRAWN STROGANOFF
Serves 4

*1¹/₂ oz (35 g) butter*
*1 large onion, finely chopped*
*4 oz (110 g) button mushrooms, chopped*
*8 oz (225 g) shelled prawns*
*5 oz (150 ml) carton soured cream*
*salt and pepper*
*tagliatelle or garlic bread to serve*

Pre-heat the oven to 400°F/200°C/Gas mark 6. Slowly cook the onion in melted butter until soft. Add the mushrooms and prawns to the pan and simmer for 2-3 minutes. Stir in the soured cream, heat gently and season to taste. Serve immediately with tagliatelle or hot garlic bread.

# CRISPY FISH KEBABS
Serves 4

*1 lb (450 g) cod, haddock or hoki fillets, skinned and cubed*
*4 oz (110 g) mushrooms, halved*
*2 courgettes, thickly sliced*
*seasoned flour*

*Batter:*
*4 oz (110 g) plain flour*
*pinch salt*
*1 level tsp dry English mustard*
*1 egg, separated*
*¹/₄ pt (150 ml) water*
*oil for deep frying*
*lemon and tomato wedges to garnish*

Finely coat the fish, mushrooms and courgettes with flour and then arrange on metal skewers. Put the flour, salt and mustard in a bowl. Blend the egg yolk with the water and beat into the flour until smooth. Whisk the egg white until stiff and then fold into the batter. Heat the oil to 375°F/190°C. Spoon the batter over the kebabs and deep-fry for 3-4 minutes. Drain on kitchen paper. Arrange the kebabs on a serving plate and garnish with lemon and tomato wedges. Serve with tartare sauce.

## PRAWN PROVENCAL
Serves 4

*1 oz (25 g) butter*
*1 small onion, chopped*
*1 clove garlic, crushed*
*1 lb (450 g) tomatoes, skinned, quartered and deseeded*
*1 small courgette, sliced*
*1 tsp chopped parsley*
*1 tbsp fresh basil*
*8 oz (225 g) peeled prawns*
*plain boiled rice to serve*

Gently cook the onion, garlic and courgette in melted butter until soft. Stir in the tomatoes and herbs, season and simmer for about 5 minutes. Add the prawns, adjust seasoning to taste and reheat to boiling point. Serve with plain boiled rice.

## DEVILLED CRAB
Serves 4

*2 oz (50 g) butter*
*1 small onion, finely chopped*
*1/2 small green pepper, seeded and finely chopped*
*2 oz (50 g) flour*
*3/4 pt (450 ml) milk*
*2 level tsp French mustard*
*1/2 level tsp mustard powder*
*1 tbsp Worcestershire sauce*
*2 tbsp chopped parsley*
*salt and pepper*
*large pinch cayenne pepper*
*4 hard-boiled eggs, chopped*
*7 oz (200 g) can crab meat, drained*
*4 level tbsp freshly grated Parmesan cheese*

Melt the butter in a pan, add the onion and green pepper and fry gently for 5 minutes until soft. Blend in the flour and cook for a minute. Stir in the milk and bring to the boil, stirring continuously until thickened. Add the mustards, Worcestershire sauce, parsley, salt, peppers and egg, and mix well. Flake the crab, remove any bones, and stir into the sauce. Heat the grill to moderate. Divide the crab mixture between 4 individual heatproof dishes, sprinkle the tops with Parmesan cheese, and place under the grill until golden brown and bubbling. Serve immediately.

# SCALLOPED ROES
Serves 4

*6 oz (175 g) roes*
*a little vinegar*
*fresh brown breadcrumbs*
*1 large tomato*
*2 oz (50 g) butter*
*finely chopped parsley*

*Oven: 350°F/180°C/Gas Mk 4*

Place the roes in a saucepan and cover with water to which a little salt and vinegar has been added. Boil gently until firm. Butter individual cocotte dishes, and sprinkle brown breadcrumbs around the inside with a layer on the base. Then make a layer of the cooked roes, season well, cover with more breadcrumbs and continue layering, finishing with a slice of tomato on top of each covered with a sprinkling of breadcrumbs. Put a few slivers of butter on top of each dish and bake in the oven until golden brown. Serve very hot sprinkled with chopped parsley.

# SMOKED MACKEREL HOT-POTS
Serves 4

*½ oz (10 g) butter*
*2 sticks celery, chopped*
*1 small onion, chopped*
*8 oz (225 g) smoked mackerel fillets, skinned and flaked*
*2 tomatoes, skinned, seeded and chopped*
*juice of ½ lemon*
*2 tbsp single cream*
*1 oz (25 g) brown breadcrumbs*
*1 oz (25 g) Cheddar cheese, finely grated*
*parsley sprigs and 4 slices lemon to garnish*

Sauté the onion and celery in the butter until soft but not brown. Meanwhile, put the smoked mackerel in a bowl and add the tomatoes, lemon juice, cream and the softened onion and celery. Season. Divide the mixture between 4 ramekin dishes. Mix the breadcrumbs and grated cheese together and sprinkle over the top of each ramekin. Place in a preheated oven (180°C/350°F/Gas Mark 4) for 20 minutes or until the topping is crisp and golden. Garnish with parsley sprigs and serve with lemon slices and thinly sliced brown bread and butter.

# LOBSTER NEWBURG
Serves 4

*about 1¾ lb (800 g) lobster*
*1½ oz (35 g) butter*
*6 tbsp medium sherry*
*¼ pt (150 ml) double cream*
*2 egg yolks*
*salt and pepper*
*cayenne pepper*
*4 small sprigs of parsley*

Ask your fishmonger to split the lobsters and crack the claws.
Remove the meat from the claws with a sharp knife. Chop the lobster
flesh, melt the butter in a shallow pan and add the lobster flesh. Cook
gently for 4 minutes, turning once. Stir in the sherry and let the mixture simmer until the sherry is reduced to 2 tbsp. Stir in all but 2 tbsp
of the cream and heat through until the mixture is just below boiling
point. Blend the remaining cream with the egg yolks and add this to
the lobster mixture. Reheat carefully to thicken the sauce slightly, but
do not allow it to boil, as it will curdle. Taste and season with salt and
pepper, then divide the lobster between 4 warm serving dishes.
Sprinkle each with a little cayenne pepper and garnish with a sprig of
parsley.

# PATES AND MOUSSES

## CHICKEN LIVER PATE
### Serves 4-6

*3 oz (75 g) butter*
*1 small clove of garlic*
*4 rashers unsmoked streaky bacon*
*1 small onion*
*pinch of celery salt or thyme*
*8 oz (225 g) chicken livers*
*1 tbsp cream*
*salt and pepper*
*small pinch of mixed spice*
*1 tbsp brandy or dry sherry*

Chop the bacon and onion into small pieces and crush the garlic.
Place in a pan together with 2 oz (50 g) of butter and cook slowly
until soft. Chop the chicken livers and add to the pan with salt and
pepper to taste. Cook gently for 5 minutes. Remove from the heat and
leave to cool, then add the cream and brandy or sherry. Pass twice
through a liquidiser or mincer. Pile into a serving dish, smooth the
surface flat. Melt the remaining butter and pour over the mixture.
Chill thoroughly.

## MAHARAJA'S MOUSSE
### Serves 6

*1 small clove garlic, crushed*
*6 oz (175 g) cream cheese*
*15 oz (425 g) can consommé*
*1 tbsp dry sherry*
*1 level tsp curry powder*
*few snipped chives to garnish*

Place all the ingredients, except the chives, into a blender or processor
and liquidise to a puree. Pour into 6 ramekin dishes and leave in the
refrigerator to set. Just before serving sprinkle the top with the
snipped chives and serve with hot toast fingers.

# DUCK TERRINE
Serves 8

*4 lb (1.8 kg) oven-ready duck*
*2 tbsp Cointreau or Grand Marnier*
*1 lb (450 g) pork fillet*
*8 oz (225 g) belly pork*
*2 eggs*
*2 level tsp salt*
*freshly ground black pepper*
*2 bay leaves*
*1 oz (25 g) butter*

*Oven: 220°C/425°F/Gas Mk 7*

Wipe the duckling and remove the giblets, if any. Reserve the liver. Prick the skin all over and put the duck on a rack in a roasting tin. Roast in a preheated oven for 30 minutes. When cool, remove all the flesh from the bones and discard the skin. Dice the breast pieces and put in a shallow dish with the liqueur. Leave to marinade for at least 1 hour. Wipe and trim the pork fillet and belly pork and cut into pieces. Pass through a mincer together with the duck liver and remaining pieces of flesh. These meats can also be processed in a food processor. Add the eggs, salt and pepper, marinaded duck flesh and the liqueur. Mix together well. Press the mixture into a buttered 2 pint (1.1 litre) terrine. Top with the bay leaves, cover with a lid or buttered foil and place in a roasting tin. Fill the tin to a depth of 1 inch (2.5 cm) with water. Cook in a preheated oven (160°C/325°F/Gas Mk 3) for 2 hours. Leave to cool overnight pressed under a weight. The next day pour melted butter over the surface and chill. Serve in slices with salad.

# TARMAKH (COD'S ROE PASTE)

*8 oz (225 g) smoked cod's roe*
*1 lemon*
*2 tbsp olive oil*
*1 onion*
*salt and pepper*
*chopped parsley*

Mash the cod's roe. Add the juice of a lemon and mix thoroughly. Add the olive oil little by little until a thick paste is formed. Season to taste. Garnish with chopped parsley and raw onion rings.

# ROAST BEEF SPREAD

*5 oz (150 g) finely chopped cooked roast beef*
*½ pt (300 ml) sour cream*
*2 tbsp chilli sauce (or to taste)*
*horseradish to taste*
*salt*
*3 oz (75 g) finely chopped onion*

Mix all the ingredients together well, chill, and serve with rye bread, pumpernickel or crackers.

# SALMON MOUSSE
## Serves 5-6

*1 pkt (½ oz/10 g) powdered gelatine*
*3 tbsp cold water*
*8 oz (225 g) can pink salmon*
*1 tbsp lemon juice*
*7 oz (200 g) jar mayonnaise*
*¼ pt (150 ml) double cream*
*sprigs of parsley to garnish*

Place the gelatine and water in a small bowl and leave for 3 minutes to form a 'sponge'. Stand in a pan of simmering water and stir until the gelatine has dissolved and is clear. Leave to cool. Drain the salmon, remove any black skin and bone and flake the flesh. Put in a bowl with the lemon juice and mayonnaise and mix thoroughly. Stir in the gelatine. Whisk the cream until thick and just forming soft peaks, and then fold into the salmon mixture, seasoning to taste. Divide the mixture between 5-6 small ramekin dishes, smooth the tops and leave to set in a cool place. Garnish with a small sprig of parsley and serve with brown bread and butter.

## LIVER AND MUSHROOM PATE
### Serves 6

*4 oz (110 g) onion, chopped*
*1 clove garlic, crushed*
*12 oz (350 g) lamb's liver, sliced*
*4 oz (110 g) streaky bacon, derinded and chopped*
*4 oz (110 g) mushrooms, washed and chopped*
*2 oz (50 g) butter*
*1½ oz (35 g) plain flour*
*½ pint (300 ml) milk*
*½ tsp dried basil*
*salt and pepper*

*Oven: 325°F/160°C/Gas Mk 3*

Melt ½ oz (10 g) of the butter in a frying pan, add the onion, garlic, liver, bacon and mushrooms and cook for 10 minutes. When cooked, remove from the pan and mince well. Add the remaining butter to the pan, stir in the flour and gradually add the milk. Bring to the boil and cook for 2 minutes, stirring continuously. Stir in the liver mixture and the basil, and add salt and pepper to taste. Place in a small terrine, cover and put in a deep roasting tin half filled with water. Bake in the oven for 1½ hours. Chill and serve.

## TUNA PATE
### Serves 6

*1 oz (25 g) butter*
*1 small onion, chopped*
*14 oz (400 g) can tuna fish, drained*
*1 tsp anchovy essence*
*2 tsp vinegar*
*6 oz (175 g) softened butter*
*salt and pepper*

Melt 1 oz (25 g) butter in a pan, and gently cook the onion until soft. Mash the tuna until smooth, stir in all the other ingredients and mix well. Adjust seasoning. Turn into a 1½ pt (900 ml) dish or terrine and chill before serving with hot toast and butter.

# SMOKED HADDOCK MOUSSE
Serves 6

*1 lb (450 g) smoked haddock*
*½ pt (300 ml) milk*
*freshly ground black pepper*
*1 oz (25 g) butter*
*¾ oz (15 g) flour*
*½ oz (10 g) pkt powdered gelatine*
*2 tbsp water*
*½ pt (300 ml) mayonnaise*
*juice of 1 lemon*
*¼ pt (150 ml) double cream, whipped*
*2 hard-boiled eggs, finely chopped*
*cucumber slices to garnish*

Gently poach the fish in the milk seasoned with back pepper until it flakes easily. Drain the fish, reserving the milk, then flake and remove all skin and bones. Make a white sauce by melting the butter in a pan, stirring in the flour and cooking for a minute before adding the flavoured milk. Bring to the boil, stirrring until thickened. Soak the gelatine in the water for a few minutes, then add to the hot sauce and stir until dissolved. Liquidise the flaked fish and white sauce together until smoothly blended. Turn into a large bowl, and, when cool, stir in the mayonnaise and lemon juice. Fold in the cream and chopped eggs. Taste and check seasoning and turn into a 2 pint (1.1 litre) serving dish. Leave to set, then decorate with slices of cucumber before serving.

# SMOKED TROUT PATE
Serves 6

*2 smoked trout*
*10 oz (300 g) butter, melted and cooled*
*4 oz (110 g) cream cheese*
*juice of ½ lemon*
*salt and pepper*

Skin and bone the trout. Put the fillets with 8 oz (225 g) of the butter, the cream cheese and lemon juice in a blender or processor and liquidise until smooth. Divide the pâté between 6 individual serving dishes and smooth the tops. Spoon a little of the remaining melted butter over the top of each and leave to set. Serve with hot toast and butter.

# ASPARAGUS AND CRAB MOUSSE
Serves 6-8

*12 oz (350 g) can asparagus*
*6 oz (175 g) can crabmeat*
*1/4 pt (150 ml) chicken or fish stock*
*1 oz (25 g) butter*
*1 oz (25 g) plain flour*
*1/2 oz (10 g) gelatine*
*3 tbsp dry white wine*
*1/2 pt (300 ml) mayonnaise*
*1/4 pt (150 ml) double cream, lightly whipped*
*lemon slices to garnish*

Drain and reserve the liquid from the asparagus and crabmeat, adding sufficient stock to make it up to ½ pint (300 ml). Melt the butter in a pan, stir in the flour and cook for 1 minute. Stir in the stock, bring to the boil and simmer, stirring for 2 minutes. Roughly chop the asparagus and flake the crabmeat. Fold into the sauce. Dissolve the gelatine in the wine over low heat, then stir into the asparagus mixture. Fold in the mayonnaise and cream. Spoon the mixture into a 7 inch (18 cm) round tin or mould and chill until set. Turn out onto a serving dish and garnish with lemon slices.

# SARDINE PATE
Serves 4

*2 x 4 oz (110 g) cans sardines, drained*
*6 oz (175 g) cream cheese, softened*
*a good pinch of finely grated zest of lemon*
*2 tbsp lemon juice*
*1 large clove garlic, crushed*
*salt and freshly ground black pepper*
*2 oz (50 g) butter, melted*

Mash the sardines with the lemon juice and zest, removing as much scale as possible. Beat in the cream cheese and season to taste. Divide between 4 cocotte dishes, level the surface and pour the melted butter over the top. Chill until butter has set. Garnish with a parsley sprig and serve with hot toast fingers.

## QUICK AND EASY FISH PATE
Serves 4

*6 oz (175 g) jar taramasalata*
*4 oz (110 g) cream cheese*
*salt and pepper*
*4 tbsp double cream*
*a little fresh lemon juice*

Mix all the ingredients together thoroughly. Place in a serving dish and chill. Serve with hot toast and butter.

## SMOKED TROUT MOUSSE
Serves 4-6

*3 smoked trout*
*1/2 pt (300 ml) dry white wine*
*2 tsp finely chopped onion*
*1/2 clove garlic, crushed*
*1 parsley sprig*
*2 tarragon sprigs*
*1 thyme sprig*
*2 bay leaves*
*10 fl oz (300 ml) soured cream*
*lemon slices and parsley sprigs to garnish*

Place the trout in a pan with the wine, onion, garlic, herbs, and salt and pepper to taste. Cover and cook gently for 10 minutes. Lift the fish from the pan, reserving the cooking liquor. Discard the skin and bones. Place the fish in a blender or food processor. Boil the cooking liquid until reduced by one third, then strain into the blender or food processor and work to a puree. Turn into a bowl and fold in the cream. Cover and chill until required. Spoon into individual dishes and garnish with lemon slices and parsley.

## KIPPER PATE
### Serves 4

*7oz (200 g) tin kipper fillets*
*1 oz (25 g) butter*
*3 tbsp double cream*
*juice of ½ lemon*
*freshly ground black pepper*

Drain the kipper fillets and break up the fish into fine flakes, removing any bones and skin. Put into a bowl with the cream, lemon juice and black pepper, add the melted butter and mix with a fork. Check seasoning and divide between four ramekins. Put into the refrigerator to set. Sprinkle a little grated lemon rind on top and serve with toast fingers or pitta bread and slices of lemon.

## NEPTUNE'S MOUSSE
### Serves 4

*4 whole large slices of smoked salmon*
*15 fl oz (450 ml) fish stock*
*5 fl oz (150 ml) dry white wine*
*12 oz (350 g) shelled prawns*
*3 oz (75 g) butter*
*4 fl oz (120 ml) double cream, whipped*
*1 tsp tomato puree*
*4 sprigs of watercress to garnish*
*hot toast fingers to serve*

Carefully line 4 ramekins with the slices of smoked salmon. Boil the stock and wine together until only 2 tbsp of thick liquid is left in the pan. Chill. Put the prawns, butter and cold reduced stock into a liquidiser and puree. Tip into a large bowl and gently fold in the whipped cream and tomato puree. Spoon into the salmon lined ramekins and fold the edges of the salmon over to cover as much of the mousse as possible. Refrigerate overnight. When ready to serve, turn out onto small plates, decorate with a sprig of watercress and serve with hot fingers of toast.

## CHEDDAR AND PRAWN MOUSSE
Serves 4

*2 eggs, separated*
*4 oz (110 g) Cheddar cheese, finely grated*
*1 tbsp freshly grated Parmesan cheese*
*2 tsp English mustard*
*cayenne pepper*
*grated nutmeg*
*10 fl oz (300 ml) double cream*
*2 oz (50 g) peeled prawns, chopped*
*whole prawns and lemon slices to garnish*

Beat the egg yolks until pale in colour. Mix in the cheeses, mustard and cayenne, nutmeg and add salt to taste. Whip the cream until it just holds its shape. Fold into the cheese mixture with the prawns. Whisk the egg whites until stiff, then fold into the mixture. Spoon into 4 ramekin dishes and chill until required. Serve garnished with prawns and lemon slices.

## SALMON AND WATERCRESS PATE
Serves 8

*6 oz (175 g) smoked salmon pieces*
*1 bunch watercress*
*6 oz (175 g) unsalted butter*
*lemon juice*
*salt and freshly ground pepper*

Roughly chop the smoked salmon. Rinse and finely chop the watercress. Beat the butter until soft and creamy and gradually beat in the salmon and watercress. Blend together thoroughly. Add lemon juice and seasoning to taste. Cover and chill overnight. Serve with toast fingers.

## SMOKED MACKEREL PATE
### Serves 6

*2 smoked mackerel*
*10 oz (300 g) butter, melted and cooled*
*4 oz (110 g) cream cheese*
*juice of 1/2 lemon*
*1 tsp horseradish sauce*
*salt and pepper*

Skin and bone the mackerel. Put the fillets with 8 oz (225 g) of the butter, the cream cheese, horseradish sauce and lemon juice in a blender or food processor and blend until smooth. Divide the pâté between 6 individual serving dishes. Spoon a little of the remaining melted butter over the top of each and leave to set. Serve with hot toast and butter.

## EGG MOUSSE
### Serves 4

*6 eggs*
*3 egg whites*
*1/4 pt (150 ml) white sauce*
*1/2 pt (300 ml) double cream*

Boil the eggs for 7 minutes and cool under running cold water. Shell and chop very finely. Make the white sauce and when cool enough mix in the eggs. Whip the cream until thick and add to the egg mixture when it is cold. Season well and add a touch of garlic or garlic powder. Whisk the egg whites until firm and fold into the mixture. Put into 4 individual dishes and chill for 4 hours.
Variation: Top with prawns tossed in mayonnaise flavoured with a little tomato puree or curry powder.

# PARSNIP PATE
## Serves 6

*1 lb (450 g) parsnips*
*1 small onion, peeled and finely chopped*
*2 tbsp walnut or olive oil*
*1 tbsp lemon juice*
*2 oz (50 g) roughly chopped walnuts*
*salt and freshly ground black pepper*
*pinch paprika*
*12 watercress sprigs*

Peel the parsnips, cut into chunks and cook in a little boiling, salted water until tender. Drain and mash. Add the onion, oil, lemon juice and half the walnuts and beat well until creamy. Season well and leave to cool. To serve, heap the mixture into a cone shape, fork over the surface and sprinkle with paprika and the remaining walnuts. Ring the base of the cone with sprigs of watercress and hand round fingers of hot toast separately.

# SMOKED SALMON PATE
## Serves 4

*8 oz (225 g) smoked salmon trimmings*
*2 oz (50 g) unsalted butter, softened*
*6 tbsp lemon juice*
*salt*
*cayenne pepper*
*1 drop Tabasco sauce*
*1 tbsp chopped chives*
*1 tbsp chopped parsley*
*lemon slices to garnish*

Remove any bones and skin from the salmon and mince or chop finely. Cream together the butter and 2 tbsp lemon juice, then beat in the salmon, and season. Add the Tabasco and remaining lemon juice and mix until the pâté is thick and creamy. Stir in the chives and parsley. Cover and chill until required. Spoon the pâté into 4 ramekin dishes and garnish with lemon slices. Serve with hot buttered toast.

# DIPS

## TOMATO AND GARLIC DIP
Serves 6-8

*1 bunch spring onions, trimmed and chopped*
*1 lb (450 g) tomatoes, skinned and chopped*
*3 cloves garlic, crushed*
*1 oz (25 g) pine kernels*
*2 tbsp olive oil*
*1 oz (25 g) fresh breadcrumbs*
*1 oz (25 g) Parmesan cheese*
*2 tsp anchovy essence*
*1 tsp paprika*
*3 tbsp tomato puree*
*Dippers: artichoke hearts; red or yellow peppers; button mushrooms*

Sauté the onions, garlic and pine kernels in the oil for 3 minutes. Add the rest of the ingredients, bring to the boil and simmer for 10 minutes stirring from time to time. Puree in a liquidiser or rub through a sieve until smooth. Season to taste. Reheat gently for about 5 minutes when ready to use. Suggested dippers are canned artichoke hearts cut into thirds, small 1 inch (2.5 cm) squares of peppers of various colours, small button mushrooms, wiped. When prepared put all these into a heatproof dish. Brush well with oil, season with salt and freshly ground pepper and put under a hot grill for about 3 minutes until heated through. Serve with crusty French bread.

## MIXED CHEESE DIP
Serves 6

*8 oz (225 g) cottage cheese*
*4 oz (110 g) Cheddar cheese, cubed*
*3 oz (75 g) cream cheese*
*8 tbsp double cream*
*salt to taste*
*1/4 tsp paprika*

Blend all ingredients until smooth. Serve with vegetable crudités or crackers.

# TUNA DIP
Serves 4

*1 x 7 oz (200 g) tin tuna, drained*
*6 tbsp mayonnaise*
*1 oz (25 g) chopped onion*
*1 oz (25 g) chopped green pepper*
*1 stalk celery, sliced*
*1 small carrot*
*1 tsp Worcestershire sauce*
*salt to taste*

Blend all ingredients until smooth. Serve with vegetable crudités or crackers.

# HAM DIP
Serves 4

*4 oz (110 g) ham, cubed*
*3 oz (75 g) cream cheese, cubed*
*1 slice onion*
*1 tbsp chopped parsley*
*1½ tsp Worcestershire sauce*

Blend all ingredients until smooth. Serve with crackers, vegetable crudités or pitta bread.

# HAM AND MUSHROOM DIP
Serves 4

*3 oz (75 g) cooked ham, cubed*
*1 x 4 oz (110 g) tin mushrooms*
*3 tbsp chutney*
*3 tbsp mayonnaise*
*¼ tsp paprika*

Blend all ingredients until smooth. Serve with vegetable crudités.

# TARAMASALATA
### Serves 4

*8 oz (225 g) smoked cod's roe*
*1 small onion, chopped*
*1/4 pt (150 ml) olive or nut oil*
*juice from 2 lemons*

Put all the ingredients into a liquidiser and blend at 3/4 of maximum speed for 5 minutes. Add more oil if the mixture is too dry. When the mixture is a smooth and creamy consistency add the lemon juice. Serve with hot pitta bread.

# ANCHOVY DIP
### Serves 4

*3 tbsp mayonnaise*
*3 tbsp double cream*
*l slice onion*
*1 tbsp chopped parsley*
*1 tbsp anchovy paste*
*6 oz (175 g) cream cheese, cubed*

Blend the mayonnaise, cream, onion, parsley and anchovy paste until smooth. Add the cream cheese, a cube at a time, and blend in until smooth. Serve with crackers.

# HOUMOUS
### Serves 6

*1 lb (450 g) chick peas*
*8 oz (225 g) Tahini paste*
*3 cloves garlic*
*3 tbsp lemon juice*

Soak the chick peas for 24 hours. Boil for about 1 hour. In a liquidiser, blend all the ingredients to a rough consistency. Add salt and pepper to taste. Serve sprinkled with paprika with hot pitta bread.

## SPICY EGG DIP
Serves 4

*5 tbsp mayonnaise*
*1 tbsp chilli sauce (or to taste)*
*salt*
*8 hard boiled eggs, chopped*
*sliced pimientos*
*stuffed olives*

Mix the mayonnaise, chilli sauce and salt. Add the eggs, pimiento and olives and blend for 30 seconds. Serve with crackers.

## SALMON DIP
Serves 6

*8 oz (225 g) cottage cheese*
*7³/₄ oz (215 g) tin salmon, drained*
*3 tbsp single cream*
*1 slice onion*
*1 tsp chopped chives*
*¹/₂ tsp paprika*
*salt and pepper to taste*
*dash tabasco sauce*

Blend all ingredients until smooth. Chill. Serve with cucumber fingers and crackers.

## AUBERGINE DIP
Serves 4

*2 aubergines (¹/₂-³/₄ lb/225-350 g)*
*juice of l lemon*
*1 clove garlic, crushed*
*1-2 tbsp olive oil*
*salt*
*chopped parsley and olives to garnish*

Prick the skin of the aubergine in a few places and then grill it until the skin is dark and blistered and the inside is tender. Peel the aubergine and put the flesh and the other ingredients into a blender or food processor. Blend until smooth. Garnish with chopped parsley and olives and serve with hot pitta bread or toast.

## CHEESE AND CHUTNEY DIP
### Serves 2

*4 oz (110 g) pkt cream cheese*
*2 oz (50 g) sweet chutney*
*1 tbsp lemon juice*
*¹/₂ tsp curry powder*
*¹/₄ tsp dry mustard*
*salt to taste*
*bananas*
*lemon juice*

Beat together all the ingredients except the bananas and lemon juice, softening with a little cream if necessary. Chill. Cut the bananas into quarters and sprinkle them with lemon juice to prevent them from turning brown. Use as dips, together with cucumber fingers and corn chips.

## AVOCADO DIP
### Serves 4

*3 avocados, peeled and cubed*
*1 medium tomato, skinned and cubed*
*1 small onion, sliced*
*2 tbsp lemon juice*
*salt to taste*
*dash of hot pepper sauce (optional)*
*2 tbsp mayonnaise*

Blend all ingredients until smooth. Chill. Serve with crackers.

## BACON DIP
### Serves 4

*6 oz (175 g) bacon, cooked and chopped*
*5 fl oz (150 ml) soured cream*
*3 tbsp mayonnaise*
*1 slice onion*
*1 tbsp parsley*

Combine all ingredients and beat well until smooth. Chill. Serve with potato crisps or crackers. This can also be used to top a baked potato.

## BLUE CHEESE AND PINEAPPLE DIP
### Serves 6

*8 oz (225 g) cream cheese*
*8 oz (225 g) tin crushed pineapple, drained*
*5 oz (150 g) blue cheese, cubed*
*1 tbsp snipped chives*

Blend all ingredients until smooth. Chill. Serve with crackers. Can also be used as a salad dressing.

## SUNSHINE DIP
### Serves 2

*3 hard-boiled eggs, chopped*
*1 x 3 oz (75 g) pkt cream cheese, cubed*
*2 tbsp single cream*
*2 tbsp mayonnaise*
*1 tsp mustard*
*1 tbsp chopped green pepper*
*1 tsp white vinegar*

Blend all ingredients until smooth. Serve on tomato slices or with vegetable crudités.

## SHRIMP DIP
### Serves 4

*1 x 5 oz (150 g) tin shrimps (drained) - or fresh shrimps*
*2 tbsp mayonnaise*
*1½ oz (35 g) Cheddar cheese, cubed*
*3 tbsp milk*
*1 small onion, sliced*
*1 tsp Worcestershire sauce*

Reserve a few shrimps for garnish. Blend all ingredients for 1 minute. Chill. Garnish with reserved shrimps. Serve with crackers and celery or cucumber sticks.

## SAUCY SARDINE DIP
Serves 6

8 oz (225 g) cottage cheese
8 oz (225 g) tinned sardines, drained
1 tbsp horseradish sauce
½ clove garlic, crushed
½ tsp Worcestershire sauce
4 tbsp mayonnaise
2 sticks celery, chopped

Blend all ingredients until smooth. Chill. Serve with celery, radish and carrot crudités.

## CAVIAR DIP
Serves 3

5 fl oz (150 ml) soured cream
3 tbsp tomato puree
1 x 2 oz (50 g) tin caviar
1 tsp Worcestershire sauce
1 tbsp lemon juice
chopped parsley to garnish

Blend all ingredients until smooth. Serve with toast triangles.

## REMOULADE DIP
Serves 6

8 fl oz (240 ml) sour cream
8 fl oz (240 ml) mayonnaise
3 tbsp chopped chives
2 oz (50 g) chopped capers
1 clove garlic, crushed
1½ tsp paprika
1 tbsp dill pickle, chopped
1 tbsp lemon juice
2 tbsp chopped parsley

Mix all the ingredients together and serve with crackers or vegetable crudités.

# CORN DIP
Serves 4

*4 oz (110 g) cottage cheese*
*8 oz (225 g) can of sweetcorn, drained*
*5 fl oz (150 ml) soured cream*
*juice of 1 lemon*
*salt and pepper*
*snipped chives to garnish*

Combine all ingredients and beat well together. Chill and garnish with snipped chives. Serve with crackers and cocktail biscuits.

# CHEESE AND CHIVE DIP
Serves 4

*4oz (110 g) low fat soft cheese*
*1 tbsp single cream*
*4 tbsp fresh chives, chopped*
*1 tbsp lemon juice*

Mix the cheese and cream together. Beat the chives and lemon juice into the cheese until well mixed. Serve chilled, with sliced vegetables and pitta bread or crackers.

# ONION DIP
Serves 4

*1 x 1 oz (25 g) pkt thick onion soup mix*
*½ pt (300 ml) milk*
*5 fl oz (150 ml) double cream*
*2 oz (50 g) ham, chopped*
*5 oz (150 g) natural yoghurt*
*2 oz (50 g) Caerphilly cheese, grated*
*sliced green olives to garnish*

Make up the soup following the instructions on the packet but using ½ pt (300 ml) milk. Cool. Whip the cream until stiff and stir into the soup with ham, yoghurt and cheese. Chill. Decorate with sliced olives and serve with crackers and sticks of carrot and celery.

## CHEDDAR CHEESE AND CELERY DIP
Serves 4

*8 oz (225 g) Cheddar cheese, grated*
*2 oz (50 g) butter, softened*
*2 level tsp mustard*
*4 oz (110 g) celery, chopped*
*5 fl oz (150 ml) double cream*
*chopped hazelnuts to garnish*

Beat the butter until smooth and stir in the cheese, mustard and celery. Gradually beat in the cream, season and chill. Sprinkle with chopped nuts. Serve with crackers.

## HERBY CHEESE DIP
Serves 4-6

*1 tbsp chopped fresh mint*
*1 tbsp chopped fresh parsley*
*8 oz (225 g) Cheddar cheese, grated*
*4 oz (110 g) cottage cheese*
*1 clove garlic, crushed*
*6 cocktail gherkins, chopped*
*salt and pepper*

Beat the herbs and cheeses together until smooth. Add the garlic, gherkins and seasoning. Chill. Serve with cucumber and celery sticks and crackers.

## CHEESE AND PEPPER DIP
Serves 4

*1 large pkt cream cheese*
*1 small can red pimientos*
*1 green pepper*
*1 clove garlic (or to taste), crushed*
*chopped olives (to taste)*

Beat the cream cheese until smooth. Finely chop the pimientos, green pepper and olives and add to the cream cheese with the garlic. If the mixture is too stiff, blend with a little double cream to correct consistency. Serve with crackers and potato crisps.

## WATERCRESS DIP
Serves 4

*8 oz (225 g) cottage cheese*
*4 tbsp milk*
*½ small onion, chopped*
*1 clove garlic, crushed*
*1 bunch watercress, washed and chopped*

Beat the cheese and milk together until the mixture is smooth. Stir in the onion, garlic and watercress. Season. Chill. Serve with crudités.

## SPICY CHEESE AND TOMATO DIP
Serves 4

*4 oz (110 g) Cheshire cheese, grated*
*2 oz (50 g) butter, softened*
*1 small onion, grated*
*1 level tsp mustard powder*
*1 tbsp tomato ketchup*
*2 tbsp single cream*
*Worcestershire sauce*
*cayenne pepper*
*chopped parsley.*

Beat together the cheese and softened butter. Stir in the grated onion, mustard powder, tomato ketchup, cream and a few drops of Worcestershire sauce. Season with cayenne pepper, mix well and chill. Garnish with chopped parsley. Serve with vegetable crudités.

## BLUE CHEESE DIP
Serves 4

*5 fl oz (150 ml) soured cream*
*1 clove garlic, crushed*
*6 oz (175 g) blue cheese, crumbled*
*juice of 1 lemon*
*salt and pepper*
*snipped chives to garnish*

Combine all the ingredients except the chives and beat together well. Do not add too much salt as blue cheese tends to be rather salty. Chill. Garnish with snipped chives. Serve with vegetable crudités or crackers.

# EGGS AND CHEESE

## BLUE CHEESE AND WATERCRESS QUICHE
Serves 6

*6 oz (175 g) pastry*
*8 oz (225 g) blue cheese, crumbled*
*1 bunch watercress, washed, trimmed and chopped*
*½ pint (300 ml) double cream*
*¼ pint (150 ml) milk*
*3 eggs*
*½ tsp grated nutmeg*
*salt and freshly ground black pepper*

*Oven: 200°C/400°F/Gas Mk 6*

Make the pastry in the usual way and use to line an 8 inch (20 cm) flan tin or ring and bake blind. Lower the oven heat to 190°C/375°F/Gas Mk 5. Beat the eggs, cream, and nutmeg together and season to taste. Stir in the crumbled cheese and the chopped watercress. Pour into the prepared flan case and bake for 35 minutes or until the custard is set and the flan is golden brown in colour.

## HERBY GOATS CHEESE WITH SUN DRIED TOMATOES
Serves 12

*2½ fl oz (75 ml) olive oil*
*2 oz (50 g) fresh basil leaves or ¾ tsp dried*
*freshly ground black pepper*
*2 oz (50 g) sun-dried tomatoes, thinly sliced*
*1 spring onion, chopped*
*12 oz (350 g) goat's cheese, sliced*
*crisp baked French bread*

In a shallow dish mix the oil, basil, pepper, tomatoes and onion. Place the cheese slices in the mixture, overlapping slightly, and spoon the mixture over the slices. Cover, and refrigerate for up to 2 days. Serve with chunks of crusty French bread.

## CREAM CHEESE AND HERB FLAN
Serves 6

*6 oz (175 g) shortcrust pastry*
*½ oz (10 g) gelatine*
*2 tbsp water*
*5 tbsp milk*
*2 oz (50 g) cheese*
*1 egg yolk*
*1 tsp mixed herbs*
*4 oz (110 g) soft cream cheese*
*½ tsp grated lemon rind*
*¼ pint (150 ml) double cream*

Prepare and cook an 8 inch (20 cm) flan case. Sprinkle the gelatine over the water in a small bowl and stir until dissolved. Heat the milk gently and stir in the gelatine. Mix the egg yolk and herbs in a bowl, season to taste and stir into the gelatine. Blend in the cheese and leave to start setting. When it is getting thick, fold in the thickly whipped cream and spoon the mixture into the flan case. Chill before serving.

## HAM STUFFED EGGS
Serves 6

*6 eggs*
*2 oz (50 g) cooked ham, finely chopped*
*4 tbsp mayonnaise*
*salt to taste*
*pinch cayenne pepper*
*strips of red pimiento to garnish*

Gently boil the eggs for 10-12 minutes. Stir the eggs for the first 8 minutes so that the yolks will be centred. Remove from the heat and plunge immediately into cold water. When the eggs are really cold, shell them and cut in half lengthwise. Remove the yolks carefully and mash them. Stir in the chopped ham with the mayonnaise and cayenne pepper. Spoon this mixture back into the egg whites and garnish with strips of pimiento.

# CHEESE BALLS IN TOMATO SAUCE
Serves 4

*8 oz (225 g) mashed potato*
*4 oz (110 g) Cheddar cheese, grated*
*2 tbsp chopped parsley*
*2 oz (50 g) flour*
*1 egg, lightly beaten*
*oil for deep-frying*

*Tomato sauce:*
*2 oz (50 g) butter*
*1 large onion, finely chopped*
*2 tbsp flour*
*4 tbsp tomato puree*
*½ pint (300 ml) chicken stock*
*1 lb (450 g) tomatoes, peeled and roughly chopped*

Mix the potato with the grated cheese and parsley. Season to taste and roll into balls the size of a walnut. Lightly roll in the flour, then coat with the egg followed by the breadcrumbs. Chill. Heat the oil and deep-fry the cheese balls until golden brown, then drain on kitchen paper. Place the cheese balls on a serving dish and keep warm. Melt the butter, add the onion and cook until soft but not browned. Add the flour and cook, stirring, for a few minutes. Gradually stir in the tomato puree and stock, bring to the boil, cover and simmer for 15 minutes. Season to taste, stir in the tomatoes and cook for 2 minutes. Pour the sauce over the cheese balls and serve immediately.

# CHICKEN STUFFED EGGS
Serves 6

*6 eggs*
*2 oz (50 g) cooked, chopped chicken*
*4 tbsp mayonnaise*
*pinch cayenne pepper*
*strips of red pimiento to garnish*

Gently cook the eggs in their shells for 10-12 minutes. Stir the eggs for the first 8 minutes so that the yolks will be centred. Remove from the heat and plunge immediately into cold water. When the eggs are really cold, shell them and cut in half lengthwise. Carefully remove the yolks and mash. Mix with the chicken, mayonnaise and cayenne pepper. Spoon back into the egg whites and garnish with strips of pimiento.

## SHRIMP STUFFED EGGS
### Serves 6

*6 eggs*
*2 oz (50 g) cooked shrimps*
*4 tbsp mayonnaise*
*2 tsp French mustard*
*salt to taste*
*pinch cayenne pepper*
*pinch of nutmeg*
*strips of red pimiento to garnish*

Gently cook the eggs in their shells for 10-12 minutes. Stir the eggs for the first 8 minutes so that the yolks will be centred. Remove from the heat and plunge immediately into cold water. When the eggs are really cold, shell them and cut in half lengthwise. Carefully remove the yolks and mash. Stir in the shrimps with the mayonnaise, cayenne pepper and a pinch of nutmeg. Spoon the mixture into the egg whites and garnish with a whole shrimp and strips of pimiento.

## FRESH HERB CHEESE
### Serves 4-6

*1 lb (450 g) carton low-fat natural yoghurt (not set variety)*
*salt*
*1 level tsp snipped fresh chives*
*1 level tsp chopped fresh tarragon*
*a few basil leaves, shredded*
*1 clove garlic*
*freshly ground pepper*
*2 tsp virgin olive oil*
*1 bunch radishes*
*black olives*
*pitta bread*
*fresh herbs to garnish*

Line a nylon sieve with clean muslin and set it over a bowl. Mix together the yoghurt and ½ level teaspoon salt. Pour into the sieve and leave in the fridge for at least 24 hours, until the yoghurt is firm and the whey has drained into the bowl. The whey can then be discarded. Turn the yoghurt into a clean bowl and mix in the herbs, crushed garlic and seasoning to taste. Transfer to a small serving bowl and drizzle over the oil. Garnish with the sprigs of fresh herbs. Serve the cheese with radishes, olives and fingers of toasted pitta bread.

## WELSH SAUSAGES
Serves 4

*1 small onion, finely chopped*
*3 oz (75 g) white breadcrumbs*
*3 oz (75 g) Cheddar cheese, grated*
*½ level tsp mixed dried herbs*
*¼ level tsp mustard*
*salt and freshly ground black pepper*
*1 standard egg*
*browned breadcrumbs*
*1 oz (25 g) butter*
*oil for frying*
*sliced tomatoes for garnish*

Mix the onion, cheese, white breadcrumbs and seasonings in a basin. Separate the egg, place the white in a bowl and mix the yolk and 1 tbsp cold water into the breadcrumb mixture. Divide the mixture into eight and roll each piece into a sausage shape. Whisk the egg white and place the browned breadcrumbs in another flat dish. Coat the sausages first in the egg white and then roll them in the browned crumbs. Chill for 5 minutes and then repeat the procedure giving a double coating. Heat the oil and butter in a frying pan and fry the sausages gently for 15 minutes, turning occasionally. Serve immediately with sliced tomato. A home-made tomato chutney goes well with this dish.

## SPINACH AND GOAT'S CHEESE
Serves 4

*8 oz (225 g) young spinach leaves, stalks trimmed*
*½ lettuce*
*4 slices white bread, cubed*
*2 cloves garlic, chopped*
*4 tbsp olive oil*
*4 Crottin goat cheeses*
*juice of ½ lemon*
*1 tbsp fresh thyme*
*salt and black pepper*

Wash the spinach and lettuce and drain well. Arrange on plates. Fry the bread and garlic in oil until golden. Remove and drain. Leave the oil and garlic to cool. Grill the cheese until browned. Arrange on the lettuce with the croutons. Blend the cooled oil with lemon juice and thyme. Season. Pour over salad and serve.

## EGGS PROVENCAL
Serves 6

*2 lb (900 g) tomatoes*
*2 tbsp oil*
*1 onion, chopped*
*1 clove garlic, crushed*
*1 bay leaf*
*2 tsp chopped fresh marjoram*
*2 tbsp tomato puree*
*pinch of caster sugar*
*salt and pepper*
*6 eggs*
*chopped parsley to garnish*

*Oven: 350°F/180°C/Gas Mk 4*

Peel and slice the tomatoes. Heat the oil in a saucepan and sauté the tomatoes, onion and garlic together for 2-3 minutes. Add the bay leaf, marjoram, tomato puree, sugar and seasoning to taste. Cover and simmer for 30 minutes, stirring occasionally, until the mixture has reduced to a thick puree. Remove the bay leaf. Spoon the mixture into six individual ovenproof dishes and place on a baking sheet. Make a hollow in the centre of the mixture in each dish and carefully break an egg into each. Season and cook in the oven for 10 minutes until the eggs are set. Sprinkle with chopped parsley and serve immediately.

## EGG MAYONNAISE
Serves 4

*4 hard-boiled eggs, shelled*
*lettuce leaves*
*salt and freshly ground black pepper*
*good quality commercial mayonnaise (or make your own)*
*small amount of double cream*
*pinch paprika*

Slice the eggs in half lengthwise. Place cut side down on lettuce leaves on individual plates. Spoon the mayonnaise carefully over the eggs to cover, and sprinkle with a pinch of paprika. If commercial mayonnaise is too thick, thin with a little double cream.

# MOZZARELLA AND RICE NUGGETS
Serves 6

*14 oz (400 g) risotto rice*
*4 eggs, beaten*
*pinch of grated nutmeg*
*3 oz (75 g) cooked ham, diced*
*3 oz (75 g) mozzarella cheese, diced*
*2 tbsp parsley, chopped*
*2 tbsp plain flour*
*6 oz (175 g) white breadcrumbs*

Cook the rice in boiling, salted water for 12 minutes or until just tender. Drain thoroughly and place in a bowl. Leave to cool for a few minutes, then stir in 2 of the eggs. Season with pepper and nutmeg and leave to cool completely. Stir the ham, mozzarella and parsley into the rice. Shape the mixture into 24 balls. Chill in the fridge for 1 hour. Dust the rice balls with the flour, roll in the two remaining eggs, then coat with the breadcrumbs. Deep-fry in batches of 8 for 3 minutes until golden and crisp. Drain and serve hot with a side salad.

# BLUE CHEESE BITES
Serves 6

*2 oz (50 g) butter*
*2 oz (50 g) plain flour*
*1/2 pt (300 ml) milk*
*6 oz (175 g) blue cheese, crumbled*
*pinch of paprika*
*4 gherkins, roughly chopped*
*1 egg, beaten*
*2 oz (50 g) dry white breadcrumbs*
*red-skinned eating apple, sliced and dipped in lemon juice.*

Make a white sauce by stirring the flour into the melted butter and cooking gently for 1 minute. Gradually stir in the milk and bring to the boil slowly. Continue to cook, stirring continuously, until the sauce thickens, then stir in the crumbled cheese and seasonings. Turn into a greased 7 inch (17.5 cm) square tin. Chill for 3 hours. Remove from the tin and cut into small cubes. Using floured hands, press a piece of gherkin into each cube,and roll in the egg and breadcrumbs to coat. Fry in oil in a deep-fryer for several minutes until golden. Lift out with a slotted spoon and drain on kitchen paper, keeping warm while cooking the remainder. Serve garnished with slices of apple.

# EGG AND CHEESE CROQUETTES
Serves 4

*5 eggs, hard-boiled*
*2 oz (50 g) butter*
*2 oz (50 g) flour*
*½ pt (300 ml) milk*
*4 oz (110 g) Cheddar cheese, grated*
*2 tbsp chives, chopped*
*6 tbsp plain flour*
*3 oz (75 g) breadcrumbs*
*oil for deep-frying*

Melt the butter in a pan. Remove from the heat and add the flour. Stir vigorously and gradually add the milk, stirring all the time until smooth. Return to the heat and gently bring to the boil. Add the cheese. Reduce heat and continue stirring until the sauce thickens. Remove from the heat and cool. Drain, shell and chop the eggs. Stir into the sauce with the chives and season. Chill for 15 minutes. With floured hands, shape the mixture into croquettes. Beat the remaining egg. Coat the croquettes in flour and brush with beaten egg. Repeat this, then roll in the breadcrumbs, ensuring all croquettes are thoroughly coated. Heat the oil until a piece of bread cooks in about 10 seconds. Carefully lower the croquettes into the hot oil and deep-fry until crisp and golden. Drain them on kitchen paper and serve hot.

# INDIVIDUAL CHEESE SOUFFLES
Serves 6

*3 oz (75 g) butter*
*4 oz (110 g) Cheddar cheese*
*1½ oz (35 g) plain flour*
*9 fl oz (270 ml) milk*
*4 eggs, separated*

Grease 6 ¼ pt (150 ml) ramekins with ½ oz (10 g) butter. Melt the remaining butter in a pan, add the flour and cook gently, stirring, for 2 minutes. Remove from the heat and blend in the milk. Bring to the boil, stirring, and simmer for about 3 minutes until a thick white sauce forms. Remove from the heat, season and stir in the grated cheese. Beat in the egg yolks, one at a time. Whisk the egg whites until stiff, then fold into the soufflé mixture until evenly mixed. Divide between the ramekins and bake in the oven at 200°C/400°F/Gas Mk 6 for 15 minutes until well risen.

# EGG FOAM
Serves 4

*6 eggs*
*3 egg whites*
*¼ pint (150 ml) white sauce*
*½ pint (300 ml) double cream*
*4 oz (110 g) prawns*
*mayonnaise*
*tomato paste*

Boil the eggs for 7 minutes and cool under cold running water. Shell and chop finely, and mix into the white sauce. Cool and then put in the refrigerator to chill. Whip the cream until thick and add to the egg mixture, seasoning well. Whip the egg whites until firm and fold into the mixture gently, making sure that they are well blended. Put into 4 individual cocotte dishes and chill. When ready to serve, divide the prawns mixed with a little mayonnaise and a touch of tomato paste between the four dishes and decorate with a parsley sprig.

# CHEESE AND MUSHROOM RAMEKINS
Serves 4

*2½ oz (60 g) butter*
*1 onion, chopped*
*1 clove garlic, crushed*
*8 oz (225 g) mushrooms, wiped and sliced*
*1 oz (25 g) flour*
*½ pt (300 ml) milk*
*2 oz (50 g) Cheddar cheese, grated*
*1 tbsp single cream*
*parsley, chopped*

*Oven: 375°F/190°C/Gas Mk 5*

Sauté the onion and garlic in 1½ oz (35 g) of the butter for a few minutes, then add the sliced mushrooms and cook until tender. Divide this mixture between 4 ramekin dishes. Melt the remaining butter in a saucepan, add the flour and cook for 1 minute, stirring continuously. Gradually add the milk, stirring, bring to the boil and cook gently until the sauce thickens. Mix half the cheese with the single cream, and season. Pour over the mushroom and onion mixture in the ramekins and sprinkle with the remainder of the cheese. Bake for 15 minutes until golden brown on top. Serve hot, sprinkled with chopped parsley.

# CHEESE CANNELLONI
Serves 4

*8 cannelloni tubes*
*1 onion, finely chopped*
*6 oz (175 g) lean bacon, derinded and chopped*
*1 red pepper, seeded and finely chopped*
*12 oz (350 g) cream cheese*
*1 clove garlic, crushed*
*2 tbsp parsley, chopped*
*3 oz (75 g) fresh white breadcrumbs*
*2 oz (50 g) Parmesan cheese, freshly grated*
*2 eggs, beaten*

Cook the cannelloni tubes in boiling, salted water and 1 tbsp oil for 5 minutes until almost cooked but still holding their shape. Drain and plunge into cold water. Re-drain. Sauté the onion in oil for a few minutes until soft but not browned. Add the chopped bacon and red pepper and cook until the pepper is soft. Put into a bowl and add the cheese, garlic and parsley. Season. Stuff the filling into the cannelloni tubes, and then coat in the beaten egg. Then roll the cannelloni in the breadcrumbs mixed with the Parmesan cheese. Repeat until all the cannelloni are coated. Heat oil in a deep-fryer until a cube of bread turns golden when dropped in. Fry the cannelloni two at a time for 2-3 minutes until golden. Drain on kitchen paper.

# EGGS WITH TUNA MAYONNAISE
Serves 4

*1 x 3½ oz (85 g) can of tuna in oil*
*juice of 1 lemon*
*black pepper*
*¼ pint (150 ml) mayonnaise*
*4 eggs, hard-boiled*
*4 lettuce leaves*
*chopped parsley and black olives to garnish*

Drain the oil from the tuna and mash the fish. Stir in the lemon juice, pepper and mayonnaise. Blend the mixture in a liquidiser or rub through a sieve to make a very smooth puree. Cut the eggs in half lengthwise and arrange yolk-side down on the lettuce leaves. Spread the tuna mayonnaise over the eggs and garnish with parsley and olives.

# DUTCH FINGERS
Serves 6

*2 oz (50 g) butter*
*2 oz (50 g) plain flour*
*¾ pint (450 ml) milk*
*pinch of nutmeg*
*6 oz (175 g) Gruyère cheese, grated*
*2 tbsp freshly grated Parmesan cheese*
*6 oz (175 g) cooked ham, finely chopped*
*2 egg yolks, beaten*
*1 egg*
*2 tbsp milk*
*fresh white breadcrumbs for coating*

Melt the butter and stir in the flour. Cook for 2 minutes, stirring. Gradually add the milk, stirring constantly. Bring to the boil, adding seasoning and nutmeg to taste. Add the cheeses and stir until melted. Remove from the heat and leave to cool slightly. Stir in the two beaten egg yolks and the finely chopped ham. Spread the mixture into a shallow baking tin in a layer about ½ inch (1 cm) thick. Cover with foil and chill for at least 4 hours. When it is thoroughly chilled and set, tip it out of the baking tin and cut into rectangles 1½ inches (4 cm) long. Beat the whole egg with the milk and dip the cheese fingers in this mixture, then coat in the breadcrumbs. Heat the oil in a deep-fryer and fry the cheese fingers until crisp and golden.

# ROASTED STILTON AND SALAD
Serves 4

*4 slices fresh French bread*
*4 oz (110 g) Stilton cheese*
*assorted salad leaves*

*Dressing:*
*1 tsp wholegrain mustard*
*2 tbsp walnut oil*
*1 tbsp port wine*
*sprinkling of chopped fresh or dried herbs*

Stir together all the dressing ingredients until they are thoroughly mixed. Cut the Stilton into 4 slices and put 1 slice on top of each piece of French bread. Heat under a hot grill until the cheese has melted. Arrange the mixed salad leaves on 4 plates and pour over the dressing. Place the cheese in the centre of each plate and serve immediately.

# VEGETABLES

## ASPARAGUS AND YOGHURT QUICHE
Serves 4

*4 oz (110 g) wholemeal breadcrumbs*
*small carton plain yoghurt*
*8 oz (225 g) fresh or frozen asparagus tips*
*3 eggs*
*¼ pint (150 ml) milk*
*4 oz (110 g) Gruyère or Cheddar cheese*

Combine the breadcrumbs with the yoghurt and season. Tip into an 8 inch (20 cm) flan dish, and press the mixture down to form an even lining on the base and sides. Lightly steam the asparagus if fresh; cook according to the instructions if frozen. Drain well. Beat the eggs, add the milk and yoghurt and season. Arrange most of the asparagus in the flan case, keeping a few pieces for garnish. Sprinkle the grated cheese over the asparagus, then pour in the egg mixture and top with the reserved asparagus tips. Bake in a preheated oven at 190°C/375°F/Gas Mk 5. for 30-35 minutes, or until set. Serve hot.

## FENNEL QUICHE
Serves 6

*6 oz (175 g) shortcrust pastry*
*1 lb (450 g) fennel*
*2 oz (50 g) butter*
*6 oz (175 g) mozzarella cheese*
*3 eggs*
*2 oz (50 g) grated Parmesan cheese*
*¼ pint (150 ml) single cream*
*chopped parsley*

Prepare and line an 8 inch (20 cm) flan tin with the pastry and bake blind at 190°C/375°F/Gas Mk 5. Trim the fennel bulbs and slice in half from top to bottom. Boil until just tender and drain well. Cut into slices and pat dry. Sauté the slices in the melted butter until they brown slightly. Put the fennel in the flan case and top with slices of mozzarella. Beat together the eggs, Parmesan and cream, and season to taste. Pour over the fennel and cheese and sprinkle with the parsley. Bake in the oven for 30 minutes until the filling is set and golden.

# BROCCOLI AND NUT QUICHE
## Serves 6-8

*6 oz (175 g) cheese pastry*
*12 oz (350 g) broccoli*
*2 oz (50 g) shelled hazelnuts, chopped*
*3 eggs*
*¹/₄ pint (150 ml) single cream*
*2 oz (50 g) Parmesan cheese, grated*

*Oven: 190°C/375°F/Gas Mk 5*

Prepare and bake blind an 8 inch (20 cm) flan case. Break the broccoli into small florets and blanch in boiling, salted water for 4 minutes. Drain and arrange on the base of the prepared flan case. Sprinkle the chopped hazelnuts over. Put the eggs, cream and seasoning in a bowl and beat well. Pour over the broccoli and nuts, sprinkle with the grated cheese and bake in a preheated oven for 20-25 minutes or until set and golden. Garnish with tomato slices and serve hot or cold.

# MUSHROOM QUICHE
## Serves 6-8

*6 oz (175 g) shortcrust pastry*
*2 oz (50 g) butter*
*1 lb (450 g) mushroms, wiped and sliced*
*1 tbsp parsley, chopped*
*1 onion, chopped*
*4 fl oz (120 ml) single cream*
*3 eggs*
*2 oz (50 g) Cheddar cheese, grated*

*Oven: 190°C/375°F/Gas Mk 5*

Roll out the pastry and line an 8 inch (20 cm) flan tin or ring. Bake blind. Sauté the onion and mushrooms gently for 5 minutes. Stir in the parsley and season to taste. Beat together the eggs, cream and cheese, and stir into the mushroom mixture. Pour into the prepared flan case and bake in a preheated oven for 35-40 minutes until set and golden. Serve hot or cold.

# HOT ONION TARTS
Makes 12

*Pastry:*
*1 lb (450 g) flour*
*8 oz (225 g) soft vegetable margarine*
*1 egg yolk*

*Filling:*
*12 oz (350 g) onions, finely diced*
*1 green pepper, seeded and chopped*
*2 tsp corn or soya oil*
*4 oz (110 g) mushrooms, sliced*
*2 eggs, beaten*
*1/2 pint (300 ml) natural yoghurt*
*4 oz (110 g) cottage cheese*

Preheat the oven to 400°F/200°C/Gas Mk 6. Place the flour in a bowl and rub in the margarine until the mixture is the consistency of breadcrumbs. Lightly beat the egg yolk together with a few tablespoons of water, then mix into the flour to make a soft dough. Roll out on a lightly floured surface. Lightly oil 12 tartlet tins, and line with pastry. Place a piece of greaseproof paper on each and weigh down with baking beans or similar. Bake in the oven for 10 minutes. Place the onions, pepper and oil in a saucepan over moderate heat and cover. Cook for 5 minutes, stiring occasionally. Add the mushrooms and continue cooking. In the meantime, mix together the eggs, yoghurt and cheese. Stir the vegetables into the cheese mixture. Remove the baking beans and greaseproof paper from the pastry cases and fill with the onion mixture. Return to the oven and cook for 20-25 minutes.

# SPINACH POTS
Serves 4

*3 eggs*
*3 oz (75 g) Cheddar cheese, grated*
*1 x 8 oz (225 g) packet frozen spinach, defrosted and drained*
*3 oz (75 g) fresh breadcrumbs*

*Oven: 375°F/190°C/Gas Mk 5*

Beat the eggs until frothy. Stir in the grated cheese, spinach and breadcrumbs. Season to taste and divide between 4 greased ramekin dishes. Bake in the oven for 20-30 minutes until risen and golden brown.

## BAKED AUBERGINES
Serves 4

*4 aubergines, with stalks removed*
*1 onion, finely chopped*
*1 clove garlic, finely chopped*
*1 tbsp olive oil*
*2 oz (50 g) fresh white breadcrumbs*
*2 anchovy fillets, chopped*
*4 black olives, stoned and chopped*
*12 tbsp chopped fresh parsley*
*1 beaten egg*

Pre-heat the oven to 350°F/180°C/Gas Mk 4. Cook the aubergines in boiling, salted water for 10-15 minutes. Drain well and halve them lengthwise. Remove all the flesh without breaking the skins, and place the flesh in a bowl. Heat the oil in a pan and cook the onion and garlic until soft and slightly brown. Mash the aubergine flesh and add the breadcrumbs, anchovies, olives and parsley. Mix into the onion and garlic in the pan, remove from the heat and stir in the egg. Season. Arrange the aubergine shells in an ovenproof dish, spoon in the stuffing and sprinkle with olive oil. Cook in the oven for 45 minutes.

## STUFFED MUSHROOMS
Serves 4

*4 large or 8 small flat field mushrooms*
*1 medium onion, finely chopped*
*2 oz (50 g) fine white or brown breadcrumbs*
*2 oz (50 g) butter*
*4 rashers streaky bacon, chopped finely*
*parsley*
*pinch mixed herbs*
*2 oz (50 g) finely grated Parmesan cheese*

*Oven: 350°F/180°C/Gas Mk 4*

Wipe the mushrooms clean and remove the stalks. Finely chop the stalks. Fry the mushrooms gently for 1 minute on each side in some of the butter. Sauté the onions and bacon pieces gently until soft, add the chopped mushroom stalks, the breadcrumbs and the pinch of mixed herbs and continue cooking gently for another minute. Pile the stuffing mix on top of the mushrooms, sprinkle with Parmesan cheese and place in a buttered ovenproof dish. Cook in the oven for 5-10 minutes. Serve hot sprinkled with chopped parsley.

# FRIED COURGETTES AND ARTICHOKE HEARTS
Serves 4

18 oz (500 g) can tomato sauce
1 tbsp chopped fresh basil or 1 tsp dried
1 tsp chopped spring onion
14 oz (400 g) can artichoke hearts, drained and rinsed
2 courgettes around 6 oz each
6 fl oz (180 ml) beer
5 oz (150 g) flour
1/2 tsp hot pepper sauce
vegetable oil for frying

In a small bowl mix together the tomato sauce, basil leaves, chopped, and sliced onion. Dry the artichoke hearts on kitchen paper and cut in half if they are large. Cut the courgettes in half and then in half lengthwise to make 4 spears. Cut each spear in half again. Pour half of the beer into a medium sized bowl and with a whisk stir in the flour and hot pepper sauce, adding more beer as necessary until the batter is light and frothy. Season. Heat the oil until a bread cube turns golden within a few moments and then, using a fork, dip the vegetables firstly into the batter and then drop them into the hot oil and fry until golden, 1-2 minutes on each side. Drain on kitchen paper, arrange in a serving dish and serve with the tomato dip.

# AVOCADO WITH ORANGE AND LIME DRESSING
Serves 4

2 tbsp fresh orange juice
juice of 1/2 lime
1 tsp sherry
1/2 tsp wholegrain mustard
2 tsp fresh coriander, finely chopped
1 small garlic clove, peeled and crushed
4 tbsp olive oil
salt and pepper
2 avocados
salad leaves to serve

Blend the juices, sherry, mustard, coriander and garlic. Season and whisk in the oil. Halve, stone and peel the avocados. Thickly slice each half, spoon over a little dressing and serve immediately with salad leaves and thinly sliced brown bread and butter.

# CAULIFLOWER, CHEESE AND MUSHROOM VOL-AU-VENT FILLING
Serves 10

*vol-au-vent cases*
*(see recipe for Savoury Vol-au-vents on page 65)*
*2 lb (900 g) cauliflower (trimmed weight)*
*2 fl oz (60 ml) dry white wine*
*1½ oz (35 g) butter*
*6 oz (175 g) onion, finely chopped*
*4 oz (110 g) mushrooms, wiped and thinly sliced*
*1½ oz (35 g) flour*
*¾ pt (450 ml) milk*
*4 oz (110 g) Cheddar cheese, grated*

Cut the cauliflower into very small florets and boil for 2-3 minutes until just tender. Drain and cool. Reduce the white wine by boiling in a small saucepan until about ½ tbsp remains. Sauté the onions and thinly sliced mushrooms in the butter and remove with a slotted spoon when softened. Stir the flour into the pan juices, and cook for 1 minute, stirring. Remove from the heat and gradually stir in the milk and reduced white wine. Bring to the boil and then simmer, stirring for 4-5 minutes. Stir in the vegetables and simmer for a further 2 minutes. Stir in the cheese and season to taste. Leave until cold before filling the vol-au-vent cases and reheating.

# MUSHROOMS A LA GRECQUE
Serves 4-6

*1 small onion, finely chopped*
*1 clove garlic, crushed*
*4 tomatoes, skinned, seeded and finely chopped*
*1 lb (450 g) button mushrooms*
*1 tbsp tomato puree*
*1 wine glass dry white wine*
*4 tbsp freshly chopped parsley*

Heat 2 tbsp oil and gently cook the onion and garlic until golden. Add the tomatoes and mushrooms and cook for 5 minutes, stirring occasionally. Mix the tomato puree with the wine and add to the pan. Bring to boiling point, remove immediately and add half the chopped parsley and plenty of black pepper. Cool. Chill for at least 2 hours and keep refrigerated until needed. Adjust seasoning and decorate with the remaining chopped parsley. Serve with crusty French bread.

# GARLIC POTATOES WITH PEPERONI

*new potatoes, scrubbed and boiled*
*mayonnaise*
*2 peperoni sausages*
*2 cloves garlic, crushed*
*gherkins*

Beat the crushed garlic cloves into the mayonnaise, or use ready made garlic mayonnaise. Slice the peperoni and mix both in with the new potatoes. Sprinkle with chopped gherkins.

## SPANISH PANCAKES
### Serves 6

*4 oz (110 g) wholemeal flour*
*1 egg*
*¼ pt (150 ml) milk*
*2½ fl oz (70 ml) water*

*Filling:*
*1 tbsp oil*
*1 clove garlic, thinly sliced*
*1 medium onion, sliced*
*½ green pepper, seeded and thinly sliced*
*6 oz (175 g) tomatoes, skinned, seeded and sliced*
*½ tsp dried mixed herbs*
*1 tbsp chopped parsley*
*1 tbsp grated Parmesan cheese*

*Oven: 400°F/200°C/Gas mk 6*

Sift the flour and a pinch of salt into a bowl, make a well in the centre and add the egg, milk and water. Beat to a smooth batter and refrigerate for half an hour. Heat a little oil in a small frying pan and pour in just enough batter to cover the base of the pan. Cook until the underside is golden, turn and cook the other side. Place on a warmed plate and cover with a tea-towel. Repeat to make 6 pancakes. Heat the oil in the pan and sauté the onion and garlic until soft. Add the remaining ingredients, apart from the Parmesan cheese, season well and cook gently for 15 minutes. Stir in the Parmesan. Divide the filling between the pancakes and roll up, tucking under the ends to keep the filling in. Place on a greased baking sheet and bake in a preheated oven for 20-25 minutes until crisp. Serve hot, sprinkled with chopped parsley.

## CELERIAC REMOULADE
Serves 4

*1 head celeriac (about 8 oz/225 g) washed, peeled and coarsely grated*
*½ small onion, finely chopped*
*8 fl oz (240 ml) thick mayonnaise*
*2 tsp lemon juice*
*1 tbsp French mustard*
*salt and freshly ground black pepper*
*lettuce leaves*
*snipped chives and lettuce leaves to garnish*

Plate lettuce leaves on each plate and sprinkle with salt and pepper to taste. Combine the remaining ingredients together in a mixing bowl, ensuring that they are thoroughly coated with the mayonnaise. Season to taste. Spoon onto the lettuce leaves and sprinkle with snipped chives.

## ASPARAGUS
Serves 4

*1 bundle fresh asparagus*
*seasoning*
*3 oz (75 g) melted butter*

To prepare the asparagus, cut away the base of the white stem so that each stalk is the right height to stand upright in the saucepan (preferably an asparagus pan). Scrape the remaining white stalk until quite green. Wash carefully in cold water. Tie into a bundle or bundles and put into boiling salted water. Cook for 15-25 minutes depending on the thickness of the stems. Do not cook too quickly otherwise the asparagus may fall over and be damaged. Drain well and serve on a hot dish with melted butter. The asparagus is held in the fingers and eaten by starting at the green tips and working downwards until the texture becomes too stringy and tasteless. Provide finger bowls filled with water and napkins on the table.
Variations:- Cook asparagus as above, and serve cold with vinaigrette dressing instead of butter.
Serve hot or cold with Hollandaise sauce.

## POTATO SKINS WITH PEPPER DIP
Serves 4

*2 lb (900 g) medium potatoes, scrubbed*
*4 tbsp oil*
*½ red pepper*
*¼ pt (150 ml) soured cream*
*¼ pt (150 ml) natural yoghurt*
*¼ tsp hot pepper sauce*

Prick the potatoes, brush with a little oil and bake them in a pre-heated oven at 400°F/200°C/Gas Mk 6 for 1 hour or until tender. Core, deseed and finely chop the red pepper. Mix in the soured cream, yoghurt and hot pepper sauce. The latter is best added a little at a time, as the flavour intensifies the longer it stands. Transfer the dip to a serving dish and refrigerate until required. Cut the baked potatoes into quarters and scoop out the flesh leaving a thick shell. Put the shells in a roasting pan, brush with the remaining oil, sprinkle with a little salt and return to the oven for 20 minutes until crisp. Put the dip bowl in the centre of a plate and arrange the hot potato skins round it.

## WALNUT STUFFED TOMATOES
Serves 6

*6 large tomatoes*
*8 oz (225 g) cream cheese*
*about 2 tbsp double cream*
*3 oz (75 g) walnuts, chopped*
*1 tbsp fresh basil, chopped*
*2 oz (50 g) sultanas*
*3 spring onions, finely chopped*
*freshly ground black pepper*

Wipe the tomatoes and cut a small slice from the top. Set aside. Hollow out the tomatoes, discarding the pips. Chop the remaining flesh. Put the cream cheese and the cream in a bowl and mix to a smooth consistency. Add the remaining ingredients, including the chopped tomato flesh, and mix well. Season to taste. Fill the mixture into the tomato shells and replace the tops. Serve on individual plates garnished with lettuce leaves. Cottage cheese can be used if preferred, omitting the cream.

# POTATO SKINS AND SOURED CREAM DIP
Serves 4

*6 large baking potatoes*
*1 tbsp olive oil*
*salt*
*oil for frying*

*Dip:*
*½ pt (300 ml) soured cream*
*1 bunch freshly chopped chives*
*2 tsp tomato ketchup*
*2 tomatoes, chopped*
*1 small green pepper, deseeded and chopped*
*1 small red pepper, deseeded and chopped*

Scrub the potatoes, rub with olive oil and sprinkle with a little salt. Bake in the oven at 400°F/200°C/Gas mk 6 for 1½-2 hours. Place half the soured cream in a small bowl and stir in most of the chives, reserving some for garnish. Season. In another bowl mix the remainder of the soured cream with ketchup and tomatoes. Season generously. Stir in most of the chopped peppers, reserving some for garnish. Heat the oil in a deep-fryer. Remove potatoes from the oven and cut into quarters lengthwise. Scoop out most of the potato, leaving a thick shell. Fry 5-6 skins at a time for 2 minutes, and drain on kitchen paper before serving. Garnish the soured cream and chive dip with the chopped chives and the tomato dip with the chopped peppers. Serve.

# BAKED GARLIC MUSHROOMS
Serves 6

*1 lb (450 g) flat field mushrooms*
*2 cloves garlic, crushed*
*3 oz (75 g) butter*
*2 tbsp chopped parsley*
*6 tbsp double cream*

*Oven: 200°C/400°F/Gas Mk 6*

Clean the mushrooms with a damp cloth and slice. Lightly grease a 1 pt (600 ml) ovenproof dish. Arrange the mushrooms in the dish. Melt the butter and add the crushed garlic cloves. Stir well and pour over the mushrooms. Combine the cream and parsley, season and pour over the buttered mushrooms. Bake in a preheated oven for 20 minutes. Serve hot with warm crusty French bread.

# VEGETABLE TARTLETS
Serves 4

*5 oz (150 g) plain flour*
*6 oz (175 g) butter or margarine*
*1 egg yolk*
*1 small onion, chopped*
*1 medium courgette, sliced thinly*
*2 oz (50 g) small mushrooms, sliced thinly*
*a little lightly beaten egg white*
*5 oz (150 g) cream cheese with herbs and garlic or fromage frais*
*2 eggs, beaten*
*4 tsp chopped basil or parsley*

Sift the flour into a bowl with a pinch of salt. Add 4 oz (110 g) of the butter in pieces and work into the flour with the fingertips. Add the egg yolk and 1-2 tsp cold water and work with a palette knife until the mixture forms a dough. Wrap the dough in cling-film or foil and chill. Melt the remaining butter in a pan, add the onion and fry gently for about 5 minutes. Add the courgettes and mushrooms and fry until golden. Meanwhile roll out the chilled dough and cut 4 circles to line individual tartlet tins. Prick the bases with a fork and cover with foil and baking beans. Bake blind at 190°C/375°F/Gas mk 5 for 10 minutes. Remove the foil and beans, brush the pastry with the egg white and return to the oven for 5 minutes. Put the cream cheese mixture in a bowl and beat until soft. Add the eggs and beat well, then stir in the courgettes, mushrooms, herbs and seasoning. Divide between the pastry cases and cook for a further 10-15 minutes, until set. Serve warm.

# CRISPY FRIED MUSHROOMS
Serves 4

*4 oz (110 g) fresh wholemeal breadcrumbs*
*1½ tsp finely chopped fresh marjoram*
*salt and pepper*
*10 oz (300 g) closed cup mushrooms*
*2 eggs, beaten*
*oil for frying*

Mix the breadcrumbs, herbs and seasoning together. Dip the mushrooms in egg, then coat with the breadcrumbs. Deep-fry in hot oil for about five minutes until golden brown. Drain on absorbent paper and serve with lemon slices, and garlic mayonnaise.

# AUBERGINE AND TOMATO LAYER
Serves 6

*4 aubergines*
*8 ripe tomatoes, thinly sliced*
*2 Spanish onions,thinly sliced*
*olive oil*
*chopped parsley and grated Parmesan cheese to garnish*

Peel the aubergines and slice thinly. Sprinkle with salt, place in a shallow dish, cover with a cloth and weight down for about ½ hr. Rinse salt off thoroughly with cold water and pat dry. Arrange the sliced vegetables in layers in an ovenproof dish, beginning and ending with onion. Season each layer with freshly ground black pepper. Pour in just enough olive oil to cover the vegetables. Bake in the oven at 250°F/150°C/Gas mk ½ for about 3 hours until all the vegetables are soft. Sprinkle with chopped parsley and grated Parmesan cheese.

# STUFFED COURGETTES
Serves 6

*6 courgettes*
*2 oz (50 g) butter*
*1 medium onion, finely chopped*
*1 red pepper, cored and finely chopped*
*3 oz (75 g) frozen peas*
*1 tsp dill*
*2 tbsp single cream*
*salt and freshly ground black pepper*
*4 eggs, beaten*

Trim the courgettes and plunge into a pan of boiling salted water. Cook for about 8 minutes or until just tender, drain and refresh with cold water for a few minutes to set the colour. Cut the courgettes lengthwise and scoop out the seeds. Meanwhile cook the onion and red pepper gently in the melted butter until soft. Blanch the frozen peas in boiling salted water for about 2 minutes, drain, and add to the onions and red pepper. Beat the dill, cream, seasoning and eggs and pour into the vegetables. Stir gently until the eggs are lightly scrambled with the vegetable mixture. Remove from the heat. Arrange the courgette halves on a serving dish and fill each one with the egg and vegetable mixture. Serve at once. This can be served on its own or with a Hollandaise or cheese sauce.

# ASPARAGUS TARTLETS
Serves 4

*5 oz (150 g) plain flour*
*4 oz (110 g) butter or margarine*
*10 oz (300 g) can asparagus pieces, well drained*
*¼ pt (150 ml) single cream*
*2 egg yolks*
*freshly grated nutmeg*

Sift the flour into a bowl with a pinch of salt. Add the butter in pieces and work into the flour with your fingertips. Add about 2 tbsp cold water and work with a palette knife until the mixture forms a dough. Gather the dough, then wrap in cling-film or foil and chill. Whisk the cream and egg yolks together and season. Roll out the dough and line 4 individual tartlet tins. Prick the bases and bake blind for about 15 minutes at 200°C/400°F/Gas mark 6. Divide the well drained asparagus tips between the tartlets and pour over the egg and cream mixture. Return to the oven and cook for about 15 minutes, or until the filling has set. Serve hot or cold with a side salad.

# CELERIAC AND TOMATO PRELUDE
Serves 4

*1 celeriac*
*6 tomatoes*
*2 tbsp fresh thick cream*
*snipped chives*
*fresh basil, chopped*
*French or Italian dressing*

*To garnish:*
*lettuce leaves*
*anchovy fillets soaked in milk,*
*mustard and cress*

Wash and peel the celeriac and shred very finely. Season with dry mustard powder. Bind with the cream. Skin the tomatoes by placing in a bowl of hot water for 1 minute, and then dice them, removing the seeds. Mix with a little French or Italian dressing to taste and sprinkle with finely snipped chives and basil. Drain the anchovy fillets. Lay the lettuce leaves on 4 individual plates and serve the celeriac and tomato mixes in alternate heaps with half an anchovy fillet on top of each. Garnish with mustard and cress.

## LEEKS A LA GRECQUE
Serves 4-6

*1 small onion, finely chopped*
*1 clove garlic, crushed*
*4 tomatoes, skinned, seeded and finely chopped*
*6 young leeks*
*1 tbsp tomato puree*
*1 wine glass dry white wine*
*4 tbsp freshly chopped parsley*

Trim the root end and remove any coarse outer leaves from the leeks. Slit the leeks down one side and wash thoroughly under cold running water to remove any grit. Heat 2 tbsp oil and gently cook the onion and garlic until golden. Add the leeks and tomatoes and cook for 5 minutes, stirring occasionally. Add all the other ingredients to the pan. Bring to boiling point, cover and simmer for about 10 minutes. Leave to cool. Chill for at least 2 hours and keep refrigerated until needed. Season and serve with crusty French bread.

## CRUDITES WITH AIOLI
Serves 4-6

*4 cloves garlic, crushed*
*1 egg yolk*
*1/2 pt (300 ml) olive oil*
*lemon juice, to taste*
*6 celery sticks, trimmed and cut into thin sticks*
*4 carrots, peeled and cut into thin sticks*
*1/2 cucumber, cut into thin sticks*
*1 red pepper, seeded and cut into strips*
*1 green pepper, seeded and cut into strips*
*6 oz (175 g) button mushrooms, wiped*
*1 small cauliflower, cut into florets*
*1 bunch radishes, trimmed*
*6 spring onions, trimmed*

To make the aioli pound the garlic in a mortar and pestle. Stir in the egg yolk. Add the oil a drop at a time, beating until the mixture begins to thicken. When the mayonnaise has started to thicken, add the oil in a thin, steady stream, beating all the time. Stir in lemon juice and season to taste. Turn into a bowl, cover and keep in a cool place. To serve, arrange all the vegetables on one large serving dish around the bowl containing the aioli dip.

# POTTED MUSHROOMS
Serves 6

*8 oz (225 g) closed cup mushrooms, very finely chopped*
*3 spring onions, finely sliced*
*4 oz (110 g) cream cheese*
*5 fl oz (150 ml) soured cream*
*1 large clove of garlic, crushed*
*salt and pepper*
*4 oz (110 g) carrot, grated*

Place the mushrooms, spring onions, cream cheese, soured cream, garlic and seasoning in a food processor and blend until smooth. Fold in the grated carrot. Turn into six individual pots and chill well. Serve with crudités and fingers of toast.

# LEEK SOUFFLE
Serves 4

*2 oz (50 g) butter*
*1 lb (450 g) leeks, thinly sliced*
*1 oz (25 g) plain flour*
*1/4 pt (150 ml) milk*
*4 1/2 oz (120 g) mature Cheddar cheese, grated*
*1 tbsp freshly grated Parmesan cheese*
*1 tsp English mustard*
*salt and pepper*
*6 eggs, separated*

*Oven: 180°C/350°F/Gas Mk 4*

Melt half the butter in a pan, stir in the sliced leeks and cook gently for 5-7 minutes or until soft but not coloured. Melt the remaining butter in another saucepan, stir in the flour and cook gently for 1 minute. Gradually stir in the milk and keep stirring while it cooks for 1 minute. Then add the cheeses, mustard, salt and pepper. Remove from the heat and then beat in the egg yolks. Stir in the cooked leeks. Whisk the egg whites until very stiff, then carefully fold into the leek mixture. Turn into a buttered 2 pint (1.1 litre) soufflé dish and bake in a preheated oven for 45 minutes until well risen and golden. Serve immediately.

# LEEK VINAIGRETTE
Serves 4-6

*12 small leeks*
*¼ pt (150 ml) olive oil*
*4 tbsp red wine vinegar*
*1 tbsp tomato puree*
*1 tbsp coriander seeds, lightly crushed*
*½ tsp sugar*
*coriander sprigs to garnish*

Top and tail the leeks. Then slit each leek lengthwise in two or three places at the top. Hold under cold running water and wash away any grit caught between the leaves. Cook the leeks in boiling, salted water for 6-8 minutes until just tender. Drain, refresh under cold running water, then leave to drain and dry on absorbent kitchen paper. To make the dressing put the oil and vinegar in a bowl with the tomato puree, coriander seeds, sugar and salt and pepper to taste. Whisk vigorously with a fork until thick. Arrange the cold leeks in a shallow serving dish and pour the dressing over them. Chill in the refrigerator for at least 30 minutes before serving. Garnish with sprigs of coriander and serve with hot garlic bread.

# ARTICHOKE HEARTS A LA GRECQUE
Serves 6

*5 tbsp olive oil*
*1 tbsp white wine vinegar*
*2 tsp tomato puree*
*1 large clove garlic, skinned and crushed*
*1½ tsp chopped fresh thyme or basil*
*6 oz (175 g) button onions, skinned*
*1 tsp caster sugar*
*8 oz (225 g) small button mushrooms, wiped*
*2 x 14 oz (400 g) can artichoke hearts*

Make the dressing: place 3 tbsp oil with the vinegar, tomato puree, garlic, thyme and seasoning in a bowl and whisk together. Blanch the onions in boiling water for 5 minutes and drain well. Heat the remaining oil, add the onions and sugar and cook for 2 minutes. Add the mushrooms and toss over high heat for a few seconds. Tip the contents of the pan into the dressing. Drain the artichoke hearts, rinse and dry. Add the artichoke hearts to the dressing and toss together. Cover and chill.

## MUSHROOMS ARDENNES
Serves 6

*6 large field mushrooms*
*3 oz (75 g) Ardennes pâté*
*1½ oz (35 g) fresh white breadcrumbs*
*2 oz (50 g) Cheddar cheese, grated*
*2 oz (50 g) butter*
*2 cloves garlic, crushed*
*parsley to garnish*

Wipe the mushrooms. Remove the stalks and chop finely. Put the pâté in a bowl and add the chopped mushroom stalks. Beat well until evenly mixed. Spoon a little of the pâté mixture into the centre of each mushroom and spread out with a knife. Mix the breadcrumbs and grated cheese. Sprinkle over the top of the pâté and press down lightly. Melt the butter in a pan. Add the crushed garlic cloves and cook for 1 minute. Season with freshly ground black pepper. Preheat the grill to a medium setting. Place the stuffed mushrooms carefully on the grill pan and spoon over garlic butter generously. Grill the mushrooms slowly for 5-6 minutes until the cheese is bubbling and golden brown. Serve the mushrooms hot with a side salad.

## ONIONS A LA GRECQUE
Serves 4

*2 lb (900 g) small onions*
*1 pt (600 ml) water*
*¼-½ pint (150-300 ml) dry white wine*
*5 oz (150 g) sugar*
*5 oz (150 g) raisins, soaked in hot water to plump them*
*4 tbsp tomato puree*
*4 tbsp olive oil*
*2-4 tbsp white wine vinegar*
*salt and freshly ground black pepper*
*cayenne pepper*
*fresh parsley, coarsely chopped*

Peel the onions and put them in a large saucepan. Add the water, dry white wine, sugar, raisins, tomato puree and oil. Add seasoning to taste, together with the wine vinegar, also to taste. Bring to the boil and then simmer gently for about ¾ hour or until the onions are tender but still retain their shape. Chill. Serve cold, garnished with chopped parsley.

# ARTICHOKES

*1 globe artichoke per person*
*melted butter*

Trim round the tops of the leaves, and cut the base so that each artichoke will stand upright. Put into boiling salted water and boil for
30-40 minutes until a leaf will pull away easily. Stand upside-down on
kitchen paper to drain. Serve each artichoke in a pool of melted butter.
To eat: a leaf is pulled off and the base is dipped in the melted butter
and then the soft flesh at the base is removed with the teeth, discarding the remainder of the leaf. When the bottom of the artichoke is
revealed the hairy centre - "choke" - is removed and the soft base or
"heart" is eaten with a knife and fork.

# SPANISH OMELETTE
## Serves 6

*1 large onion, finely chopped*
*1 large clove garlic, finely chopped*
*4 oz (110 g) cold cooked potatoes, diced*
*2 oz (50 g) red pepper, skinned and finely chopped*
*4 eggs*
*2 tbsp double cream*
*salt and freshly ground black pepper*
*vegetable oil*

Heat the oil in a frying pan, add the onion and garlic and sauté gently
until soft but not browned. Add the chopped red pepper and soften
slightly. Add the diced, cooked potato and heat through. Lightly beat
the eggs together with the cream and plenty of seasoning and pour
over the vegetables. Cook gently until the underside is firm and gold-
en brown. Put the whole pan under a preheated grill to cook the top
which should still be soft and slightly runny. Slide out onto a hot
plate and cut into wedges. Serve one slice to each person with a crisp
green salad on the side.

# HERB AND GARLIC MUSHROOMS
Serves about 6 depending on size of the mushrooms

*1 lb (450 g) medium sized mushrooms*
*2 packets Boursin herb cheese or 1 herb and 1 garlic cheese*
*2 oz (50 g) fresh white fine breadcrumbs*
*salt and freshly ground black pepper*
*1 egg*
*1 tbsp freshly grated Parmesan cheese*

*Oven: 350° F/180 °C/Gas Mk 4*

Trim the mushroom stalks and mince the stems. Wipe the mushroom caps and arrange in a lightly oiled baking dish. In a bowl mix together the Boursin cheese, the breadcrumbs, the minced mushroom stems and the beaten egg, and season well. Spoon the mixture into the mushroom caps and sprinkle with the grated Parmesan. Bake for 20 minutes until golden. This can be served hot or cold.

# AUBERGINES WITH WALNUT SAUCE
Serves 4

*4 aubergines, sliced*
*salt*
*5 dessertspoons flour*
*3 fl oz (90 ml) olive oil*
*1 onion, peeled and chopped*
*2 garlic cloves, peeled and chopped*
*3 tomatoes, peeled and chopped*
*2 tbsp chopped parsley*
*6 walnuts, finely chopped*

Soak the aubergine slices in salted cold water for 30 minutes. Drain and dry well. Flour the aubergine slices and fry in the hot oil for 3 minutes, turning once. Remove and set aside. Add the onion, garlic, tomatoes and parsley to the pan and cook for 5 minutes, stirring occasionally. Return the aubergines to the pan with the chopped walnuts. Mix together well and cook for 10 minutes.

# FRUIT

## TRICOLOUR MELON MEDLEY
### Serves 4-6

*1 Charentais melon*
*1 Ogen melon*
*½ small water melon*
*½ pt (300 ml) Greek strained yoghurt or crème fraîche*
*2 oz (50 g) almond flakes*

Halve the Charentais and Ogen melons and scoop out the seeds. Cut the flesh into ½ inch (1.25 cm) cubes or, if you have a melon baller, scoop out small melon balls, as this gives a better effect. Mix together with the water melon from which the seeds should also be removed. Pile into individual dishes. Toast the almond flakes under the grill until golden and leave to cool for a few minutes. When ready to serve swirl the greek yoghurt or crème fraîche on top of each dish and sprinkle over the toasted almond flakes.

## ORANGE AND APRICOT MEDLEY
### Serves 6

*1 x 15 oz (425 g) can apricots*
*3 large oranges*
*natural Greek yoghurt*
*dash of Grand Marnier or Orange Curacao (optional)*
*sprig of mint*

Drain the apricots and cut each half into three slices. Peel the oranges and, with a sharp knife, cut away the flesh from the surrounding pith. Mix the orange segments and apricot slices adding a little of the apricot juice mixed with a little Grand Marnier or Orange Curacao if desired. Chill well and serve with a whirl of natural yoghurt topped with a sprig of mint.

## AVOCADO WITH GRAPEFRUIT AND ORANGE
Serves 4

*2 avocado pears*
*4 tsp lemon juice*
*1 orange*
*1 grapefruit*
*4 black grapes*
*mint leaves to garnish*

Cut the avocado pears in half and remove the stones. Rub the lemon juice over the cut sides of the avocados to prevent them from browning. Peel the orange and grapefruit and cut out the flesh segments removing all pith. Remove the pips from the grapes. Arrange alternating segments of orange and grapefruit on top of the avocados, pouring any juice over them. Garnish with grapes and mint leaves.

## GRILLED GINGER GRAPEFRUIT
Serves 4

*2 pink fleshed grapefruit*
*small jar stem ginger in syrup, chopped*
*4 tsp soft brown sugar*

Cut the grapefruit in half and loosen the flesh. Cut between the segments and remove the pith and white skin. Put 1 tbsp of the ginger in syrup over each grapefruit half and sprinkle generously with sugar. Place under a hot grill for a couple of minutes until bubbling. Serve immediately.

## GRILLED SPICED GRAPEFRUIT
Serves 4

*2 large grapefruit (pink if possible)*
*4 tbsp soft light brown sugar*
*2 tbsp butter, softened*
*2 tbsp sweet vermouth*
*1/2 tsp ground cinnamon*

Cut the grapefruit in half, loosen the segments with a knife and remove any pips. Mix the topping ingredients together and spread over the top of each grapefruit. Place under a preheated grill and cook until bubbling. Put into individual dishes and serve immediately.

## PINEAPPLE SURPRISE

*2 pineapple rings per person*
*cream cheese*
*natural yoghurt*
*2 limes*
*sprigs of mint*

Beat the cream cheese with enough natural yoghurt to give a smooth piping consistency. Place two pineapple rings on each plate and pipe a swirl of cream cheese in the centre. Garnish with a slice of fresh lime and a couple of mint leaves. A little paprika may be sprinkled on top if desired.

## WILLIAM PEARS WITH STILTON
### Serves 4

*4 ripe William pears*
*6 oz (175 g) Stilton cheese*
*mayonnaise*
*lettuce leaves*

Make this dish just before serving. Peel the pears and cut in half. Take out the core. Lay lettuce leaves (radiccio and green lettuce leaves together make a pretty base) on individual plates. Lay the pears on top and pile the crumbled Stilton into the cavity where the core was removed. Serve with mayonnaise.

## MELON AND GINGER CUPS
### Serves 4

*2 Ogen melons*
*4 oz (110 g) stem ginger, diced*
*4 tbsp ginger syrup or ginger wine*
*caster sugar*

Cut the melons in half and scoop out the seeds. Remove as much flesh from the melons as possible and cut into small cubes. Mix together with the stem ginger, ginger syrup and sugar, cover and leave in the fridge for about 20 minutes for the flavours to combine. Stir and replace in melon shells to serve.

# PASTA

## MACARONI WITH SAUSAGE AND ARTICHOKES
### Serves 4

*9 oz (275 g) fluted macaroni*
*1 tin artichoke hearts*
*4 tbsp olive oil*
*2 tbsp onion, chopped*
*4 oz (110 g) spicy Italian sausage*
*½ fresh red chilli*
*4 tbsp white wine*
*salt and freshly ground black pepper*
*2 tbsp grated Parmesan cheese*

Sauté the onion in the olive oil until soft and just golden. Skin the spicy sausage and chop into small pieces. Add to the onions. Cut the artichoke hearts into quarters and add to the pan with the very finely chopped chilli pepper. The chilli pepper should be added to taste because it can be quite hot. Add the white wine and cook for 5 minutes, stirring gently. Add a few tablespoons of boiling water and mix well. Cook the macaroni in boiling salted water until al dente. Blanch and drain. Mix the pasta into the sauce, season well and add the grated Parmesan. Gently reheat and pour into a serving dish.

## SPAGHETTI WITH PESTO
### Serves 4

*4 oz (110 g) basil leaves*
*2 garlic cloves, peeled and roughly chopped*
*pinch of salt*
*2 oz (50 g) grated goat's cheese*
*1½ oz (35 g) grated Parmesan cheese*
*4 fl oz (120 ml) oil*
*14 oz (400 g) spaghetti*

Pound together the basil, garlic and salt with a pestle and mortar. Gradually add half the goat's cheese and all the Parmesan and mash together well. Gradually add the oil, stirring constantly. Cook the spaghetti in boiling salted water, drain and sprinkle with the remaining goat's cheese. Stir in the basil sauce and serve immediately.

## PASTA AND CHICKEN SCALLOPS
Serves 4

*6 oz (175 g) quick-cook short macaroni*
*3 tbsp oil*
*1 large onion, chopped*
*4 rashers back bacon, chopped*
*6 oz (175 g) button mushrooms, sliced*
*7 fl oz (210 ml) double cream*
*6 oz (175 g) cooked chicken, chopped*
*2 tbsp parsley, chopped*
*4 tbsp fresh white breadcrumbs*
*2 oz (50 g) Cheddar cheese, grated*

Cook the macaroni in a large pan of boiling salted water and 1 tbsp
oil for about 8 minutes until just tender. Sauté the onion and bacon in
the remaining oil for 2 minutes. Add the mushrooms and cook for a
further 3 minutes. Stir in the cream, chopped chicken, parsley and
macaroni and season well. Spoon into individual ovenproof dishes.
Sprinkle with the mixed breadcrumbs and grated cheese, dot with
butter and brown under the grill. Serve hot.

## VERMICELLI WITH CHICKEN LIVERS
Serves 4

*3 tbsp olive oil*
*1 onion, chopped*
*2 cloves garlic, chopped*
*1½ lb (675 g) ripe tomatoes, peeled and chopped*
*some parsley, thyme and marjoram (fresh or dried)*
*a small glass of red wine*
*1 lb (450 g) vermicelli*
*12 oz (350 g) chicken livers*
*2 oz (50 g) butter*

In a large, shallow saucepan, heat the olive oil and add the onion and
garlic. Cook very gently for 15 minutes until the onion is soft. Add
the tomatoes, pour in the wine and season with salt and pepper to
taste. Add plenty of chopped herbs and simmer over low heat for
1 hour until the sauce is thick. Cook the vermicelli in boiling water
until soft. Whilst it is cooking, chop up the chicken livers into small
pieces and sauté in butter for a few minutes until brown on all sides.
Mix into the tomato sauce. Drain the vermicelli and place in a warm
serving dish. Pour the sauce over the top and serve at once.

## VERMICELLI WITH MUSSELS
Serves 4

*1 lb (450 g) vermicelli*
*2 lb (900 g) fresh mussels*
*1 onion, finely chopped*
*2 cloves garlic, chopped*
*1 lb (450 g) tomatoes, skinned and chopped*
*3 tbsp olive oil*

Thoroughly wash and clean the mussels. Place in a large saucepan containing plenty of salted water. Boil for 5 minutes, shaking the pan from time to time. When the shells open, remove the mussels from the heat immediately. Discard any mussels which do not open when tapped sharply. Drain and remove the mussels from their shells. Heat the oil in a frying pan, add the onion and garlic and cook until soft. Stir in the tomatoes, season to taste and cook over low heat for 40 minutes. Cook the vermicelli in boiling water until soft. Drain well and place in a warm serving dish. Meanwhile, add the mussels and parsley to the frying pan and cook in the sauce until the mussels are heated through. Pour the sauce over the vermicelli and serve at once.

## PASTA WITH SALMON AND BROCCOLI
Serves 4

*8 oz (225 g) broccoli florets*
*2 oz (50 g) butter*
*1 oz (25 g) plain flour*
*15 oz (425 g) can pink salmon, drained, boned and flaked (reserve juices)*
*³/₄ pt (450 ml) semi-skimmed milk*
*4 oz (110 g) mature Cheddar cheese, grated*
*6 oz (175 g) pasta shells, cooked*

Cut the broccoli into small florets, and chop the stems into very small pieces after removing any woody skin. Melt half the butter in a pan and add the broccoli. Cover the pan and leave to sweat over low heat until tender. Remove from the pan with a slotted spoon and put on one side. Cook the pasta in a large pan of boiling, salted water. Melt the remaining butter in the pan in which the broccoli was cooked, and mix in the flour, stirring all the time, to make a roux. Make the juice from the salmon up to ³/₄ pt (450 ml) with the milk and gradually blend this into the roux, stirring continuously, until the sauce thickens. Add the cheese and plenty of pepper. Add salt to taste. Stir in the flaked salmon and broccoli. Mix with the hot cooked pasta, and serve.

# SPAGHETTI WITH FENNEL AND SARDINE SAUCE
### Serves 4

*1 lb (450 g) spaghetti*
*4 tbsp olive oil*
*6 oz (175 g) dried breadcrumbs*
*1 tbsp pine nuts or blanched almonds*
*1 lb (450 g) fennel*
*1 large onion*
*1 lb (450 g) fresh sardines*
*1 tbsp seedless raisins*

Clean and bone the fish. Clean the fennel, cut into quarters and cook for 15 minutes in just enough boiling salted water to cover. Drain and chop finely. Sauté the onion in the olive oil until it is golden, add the fish and cook gently for 10 minutes, stirring frequently. Add the fennel, nuts, sultanas and ½ pt (300 ml) cold water. Season well and simmer gently for 10 minutes. Place the breadcrumbs under the grill for a few seconds to brown. When the spaghetti is cooked, drain well and place in a deep warmed dish. Pour over the fish and fennel sauce and top with breadcrumbs. Serve very hot.

# PASTA MARINA
### Serves 6

*12 oz (350 g) pasta quills*
*3 tsp olive oil*
*8 squid rings, ready prepared*
*3 oz (75 g) shelled mussels*
*½ onion, peeled and finely chopped*
*1 clove garlic, crushed*
*4 tomatoes, peeled and chopped*
*1 tsp brown sugar*
*2 oz (50 g) shelled prawns*
*3 oz (75 g) shelled clams*
*3 tbsp dry white wine*
*chopped spring onions and prawns to garnish*

Boil the pasta in salted water with a dash of oil until just tender. Drain and cool. Heat the oil in a large pan and fry the squid and mussels for 2 minutes. Add the onion, garlic, tomatoes, sugar, seasoning, prawns, clams and wine. Simmer for 10 minutes until slightly thickened. Cool. Toss the pasta in the sauce and garnish with spring onions and prawns.

## SPINACH AND RICOTTA CANNELLONI
Serves 3-4

*9 oz (250 g) cannelloni*

*White sauce:*
*1 oz (25 g) butter*
*1 oz (25 g) flour*
*1/2 pt (300 ml) milk*

*Filling:*
*1 lb (450 g) spinach*
*4 oz (110 g) ricotta cheese*
*grated nutmeg*

Make a white sauce by melting the butter in a small pan, stir in the flour and cook for 1 minute. Gradually stir in the milk and cook, stirring continuously, until thickened. Gently cook the spinach with the grated nutmeg, salt and pepper. Drain thoroughly and mix together with the ricotta cheese. Spoon into 12 uncooked cannelloni. Place in a long, buttered, ovenproof dish and cover with the white sauce. Sprinkle with parmesan cheese, cover with foil and bake for 30 minutes at 180°C/350°F/Gas Mark 4, removing the foil after 15 minutes.

## PENNE WITH PEPPERS AND COURGETTES
Serves 4

*10 oz (300 g) fluted penne*
*1 sweet yellow pepper*
*2 small courgettes*
*1 1/2 oz (35 g) butter*
*8 oz (225 g) freshly made tomato sauce*
*1 oz (25 g) flour*
*5 fl oz (150 ml) vegetable oil*
*1 tbsp freshly chopped parsley*

Put the pepper under the grill until it blisters, then skin. Halve, deseed and cut into strips. Then dice. Also dice the courgettes. Melt the butter in a large frying pan and sauté the diced pepper for 5 minutes. Add the diced courgettes, season and fry gently until the vegetables are tender but not too soft. Add to the tomato sauce and heat gently. Put the penne into plenty of boiling salted water and cook for 10-12 minutes. Drain well and put into individual serving dishes. Pour over the vegetable and tomato sauce and sprinkle with chopped parsley and freshly ground black pepper. Hand round grated Parmesan cheese.

# PASTA SHELLS WITH WALNUT SAUCE
Serves 4

*8 oz (225 g) pasta shells*
*butter*
*12 oz (350 g) can asparagus, drained and sliced*

*Sauce:*
*4 tbsp walnut oil*
*2 garlic cloves, crushed*
*4 tbsp chopped parsley*
*3 oz (75 g) walnuts, finely ground*
*2 oz (50 g) pine nuts or cashew nuts, finely ground*
*1/4 pt (150 ml) hot water*
*1 egg, beaten*
*2 tbsp single cream*
*asparagus spears or walnut halves to garnish*

Place 3 pints (1.5 litres) water, some salt and 1 tbsp oil in a large pan and bring to the boil. Add the pasta shells, reduce the heat slightly and cook for 10 minutes, until the pasta is tender. Drain, rinse with hot water and drain again thoroughly. Melt a little butter in the pan and toss the pasta to coat evenly. Add the asparagus and stir the mix ture well. Heat the oil in a frying pan, add the garlic and parsley and fry for 1 minute. Add the nuts and fry gently until golden brown, then remove from the heat. Stir together the hot water, egg and cream until well blended. Then add to the nut mixture and stir well to blend. Spoon over the pasta and toss well. Place the mixture on a warmed serving plate and garnish with asparagus spears or walnut halves. This sauce will keep for 3 days in a refrigerator. Reheat it gently.

# TAGLIATELLE WITH GARLIC CREAM SAUCE
Serves 4

*8 oz (225 g) tagliatelle, freshly cooked*
*1/2 oz (10 g) butter*
*1 large clove garlic, crushed*
*1/4 pt (150 ml) double cream*
*1 tbsp fresh parsley, chopped*
*salt and freshly ground black pepper*

Fry the garlic clove gently in the melted butter for 2-3 minutes. Stir the cream into the pan together with the chopped parsley. Season to taste. Toss the freshly cooked tagliatelle in the sauce and serve imme-diately.

## SPAGHETTI WITH HERBED GARLIC OIL
Serves 4

*3 pints (1.5 litres) water*
*1tsp salt*
*1 tbsp vegetable oil*
*8 oz (225 g) plain or wholewheat spaghetti*
*4 lemon wedges, to garnish*

*Dressing:*
*3 tbsp olive oil*
*2 garlic cloves, crushed*
*4 tbsp of any chopped herbs in season*
*black pepper*

Bring the water to the boil in a large saucepan, adding salt and oil. Add the spaghetti, keeping the water boiling. Reduce the heat slightly and cook for 8-10 minutes, stirring occasionally, until tender. Drain, rinse with hot water and drain again in a sieve. Place the dressing ingredients in the saucepan. Replace the spaghetti and toss well to coat evenly. Place in a warmed serving dish with wedges of lemon.

## FETTUCCINE WITH CREAM SAUCE AND MUSHROOMS
Serves 4

*1 lb (450 g) fettuccine*
*½ Spanish onion, finely chopped*
*butter*
*4 oz (110 g) mushrooms, sliced*
*4 oz (110 g) ham, diced*
*¼ pt (150 ml) double cream*
*2 egg yolks*
*freshly grated Parmesan cheese*
*salt and freshly ground black pepper*

Sauté the onion in 2 tbsp butter until tender. Add the sliced mushrooms and diced ham and continue cooking gently until the mushrooms are tender, stirring occasionally. Combine the double cream, egg yolks, 4 oz (110 g) butter and freshly grated Parmesan, to taste, in the top of a double saucepan, and cook over hot water, stirring constantly with a wooden spoon, until the sauce is thick and creamy. Season to taste. Pour the sauce over the freshly cooked and drained fettuccine in the serving dish. Place the onion, mushrooms and ham on top and serve with a bowl of grated Parmesan.

# SALADS

## SPANISH HAM SALAD
Serves 4

*8 oz (225 g) ham*
*1 onion*
*4 tomatoes*
*1 green pepper*
*2 tbsp oil*
*1 tbsp vinegar*
*1 clove garlic, crushed*
*salt and pepper*

Cut the ham into strips and slice the onion into rings. Cut the tomatoes in quarters and the pepper into rings, discarding the seeds. Place in a large bowl. Mix together the oil and vinegar. Add the garlic and season with salt and pepper to taste. Pour over the tomatoes, pepper, ham and onion and toss well before serving.

## RICE AND SCAMPI SALAD
Serves 4

*4 oz (110 g) long-grain rice*
*salt and pepper*
*pinch of nutmeg*
*2 tbsp olive oil*
*squeeze of lemon juice*
*1/2 small onion, finely chopped*
*4 oz (110 g) cooked green peas*
*16 scampi*
*2 tbsp fresh parsley, finely chopped*

Place the rice in a saucepan of boiling, salted water and when it is cooked, drain well. Season with nutmeg, salt and pepper to taste. Mix in the oil and lemon juice. Add the onion and set the mixture aside to cool. When it is completely cold, mix in the peas, scampi and parsley and arrange on a serving dish.

# ARTICHOKE SALAD
Serves 4

*1 lettuce, shredded*
*1 x 14oz (400 g) can artichoke hearts, drained*
*4 oz (110 g) Mortadella sausage, sliced*
*black olives*
*4 tbsp olive oil*
*3 tbsp lemon juice*
*1 clove garlic, crushed*
*salt and pepper*

Put the lettuce in a serving bowl and arrange the artichoke hearts, Mortadella and olives on top. In a bowl, mix the olive oil, lemon juice and garlic and add salt and pepper to taste. Whisk until well combined. Pour over the salad and serve.

# SUNRISE PASTA
Serves 4

*2¹/₂ large oranges*
*3 oz (75 g) pasta shells*
*4 oz (110 g) peeled prawns*
*8 oz (225 g) broccoli florets*
*¹/₄ cucumber, diced*

*Dressing:*
*5 fl oz (150 ml) carton soured cream or Greek yoghurt*
*1 tbsp mayonnaise*
*juice of half an orange*
*few drops Worcestershire sauce*
*salt and freshly ground black pepper*
*8 prawns in shells to garnish*
*fresh parsley, finely chopped*
*pinch paprika*

Cook the pasta in boiling salted water for 10-12 minutes until al dente. Rinse under cold water. Boil the broccoli florets for 15 minutes until just tender. Leave to cool. Cut the oranges in half and scoop out the flesh. Remove the pith and chop the flesh. Serrate the rim of each orange half. Mix together the chopped orange flesh, pasta, prawns, broccoli and diced cucumber. Mix the sauce ingredients together and add to the prawn mixture. Pile into each orange half and garnish with the whole prawns, chopped parsley and a sprinkling of paprika.

## DRESSED GOUDA AND SALAMI
Serves 4

*8 oz (225 g) Gouda cheese*
*4 oz (110 g) finely sliced German or Italian salami*
*5 tbsp grapeseed oil*
*2 tbsp fresh lemon juice*
*2 level tsp chopped parsley*
*few leaves of tarragon (optional)*

Cut the cheese into fine sticks and shred the salami. Place both in a bowl. Whisk together the oil, lemon juice, parsley and snipped tarragon and season to taste. Toss together all the ingredients and leave in a cool place for 30 minutes before serving.

## CUCUMBER AND GRAPEFRUIT SALAD
Serves 4

*2 grapefruit*
*¼ cucumber*
*2 oz (50 g) diced Cheddar cheese*
*5 fl oz (150 ml) natural yoghurt*

Cut the grapefruit in half and remove the segments. Discard all pith and chop up the fruit. Dice the cucumber. Mix all the ingredients together with the yoghurt and fill the halved grapefruit shells. Serve chilled.

## TUSCAN SALAD
Serves 4

*1 lettuce*
*1 x 15 oz (425 g) can cannellini beans*
*½ onion, thinly sliced*
*3 tomatoes, skinned and quartered*
*3 tbsp olive oil*
*2 tbsp wine vinegar*
*1 x 7 oz (200 g) can tuna fish, drained*

Place the lettuce on a serving dish. Drain the beans, put in a bowl and mix in the onion and tomatoes. In another bowl, whisk together the oil and vinegar and pour over the onion and tomatoes. Toss well and arrange on top of the lettuce. Place the tuna chunks on top and serve.

## ITALIAN MEAT SALAD
### Serves 4

*1 oz (25 g) parsley, finely chopped*
*1 oz (25 g) spring onions, finely chopped*
*1 clove garlic, finely chopped*
*2 tomatoes, skinned and chopped*
*2 tbsp capers, finely chopped*
*1 oz (25 g) fresh white breadcrumbs*
*4 fl oz (120 ml) olive oil*
*4 tbsp lemon juice*
*salt and pepper*
*12 oz (350 g) sliced cooked cold meat*
*4 tbsp single cream*

Place the parsley, onions, garlic, tomatoes and capers in a bowl. Mix in the breadcrumbs, oil and lemon juice, and add salt and pepper to taste. Arrange the meat on a serving dish and pour over the sauce. Cover and set aside in a cool place for about 1 hour. Before serving, lightly swirl the cream on top.

## HERRING AND APPLE SALAD
### Serves 4

*5 fl oz (150 ml) soured cream*
*4 tbsp natural yoghurt*
*1 large, crisp, red-skinned apple*
*4 pickled herrings, drained and cut into 1 in pieces*
*½ Spanish onion, thinly sliced*
*salt and pepper*
*watercress sprigs to garnish*
*2 hard-boiled eggs to garnish*
*snipped chives to garish*

Blend together the soured cream and yoghurt in a bowl. Quarter and core but do not peel the apple. Cut the apple into thin slices and add to the bowl. Add the herrings and onion and toss gently. Season with salt and pepper to taste, cover and chill. Arrange the watercress around the edge of a serving dish. Toss the salad once more and pile in centre of the dish. Arrange the eggs around the edge of the salad and sprinkle with chives.

# TOMATO AND MOZZARELLA SALAD
Serves 4

*1 Mozzarella cheese*
*4 large, firm tomatoes*
*fresh basil, chopped*
*1 tbsp olive oil*
*1 tbsp vinegar*
*salt and pepper*

Slice the cheese and tomatoes in rounds. Arrange them in an alternating pattern on a serving dish and sprinkle over the basil. In a small bowl, mix together the oil and vinegar with salt and pepper to taste and serve the dressing separately.

# AVOCADO AND SHELLFISH SALAD
Serves 4

*2 avocado pears*
*1 can crabmeat*
*6 oz (175 g) shelled prawns*
*2 tbsp celery, finely chopped*
*1/2 tbsp tomato puree*
*4 tbsp mayonnaise*
*few drops Tabasco sauce*
*lemon juice*
*salt*

*To serve:*
*lettuce leaves*
*paprika*

Halve the avocado pears, remove the stones and sprinkle with lemon juice. Mix together all the other ingredients, adding Tabasco sauce, salt and lemon juice to taste. Chill. Pile the filling into the centres of the avocado pears and sprinkle with paprika. Serve on a bed of shredded lettuce. Alternatively, peel the avocado pears and slice the flesh. Arrange in a fan shape on the plate and place a portion of the shellfish mixture beside them. Do this at the last minute before serving. Sprinkle with paprika pepper.
Variation: Fill the avocado pear centres with diced blue cheese, Cheddar cheese and Leicester cheese mixed with the above dressing. Omit the tomato puree and sprinkle with chopped parsley.

# WATERCRESS, CROUTON AND FETA SALAD
### Serves 4

*2 large bunches of watercress*
*1 small lettuce*
*3 tbsp polyunsaturated oil*
*1 tbsp lemon juice or white wine vinegar*
*salt and pepper*
*5 oz (150 g) feta cheese*
*3 oz (75 g) packet garlic croutons*

Divide the watercress into sprigs and tear the lettuce leaves into large pieces. Wash well and refrigerate in polythene bags until required. Whisk together the oil, lemon juice or vinegar and seasoning in a large bowl. Cube the cheese. Just before serving toss together the watercress, lettuce, dressing and cheese and garnish with croutons.

# FENNEL AND TOMATO WITH LEMON AND GARLIC DRESSING
### Serves 6

*12 oz (350 g) fresh fennel (two or three heads)*
*2 tbsp lemon juice*
*3 tbsp grapeseed oil*
*1/2 level tsp garlic puree*
*salt and pepper*
*12 oz (350 g) tomatoes*
*black olives*

Trim and finely slice the fennel. Place in boiling water and simmer until soft - about 5 minutes. Mix together the lemon juice, grapeseed oil and garlic. Season to taste. Drain the fennel and immediately pour over the lemon dressing. Leave to cool. Slice the tomatoes and arrange on a serving dish. Top with fennel, pour over the dressing and garnish with a few olives. Serve cool but not chilled.

# TOMATO HEDGEHOGS

*1 large tomato per person*
*salami*
*hard boiled eggs*
*slices of cooked ham*
*slices of Edam or similar hard cheese*

*Dressing:*
*juice of ½ lemon*
*1 tbsp salad oil*
*1 tsp finely chopped fresh basil*
*1 spring onion, finely chopped*
*salt and freshly ground black pepper*
*finely chopped parsley*

Place the tomatoes stalk side down and with a very sharp knife make six cuts downwards across the tomato. Put a slice of hard-boiled egg, salami, cheese and ham alternately in the cuts. Whisk together all the dressing ingredients apart from the parsley, and pour over the tomatoes. Chill until required.

# SPINACH SALAD WITH GARLIC MUSHROOMS

*12 oz (350 g) small new potatoes, scrubbed, halved, cooked and cooled*
*4 eggs, hard-boiled and cooled*
*3 oz (75 g) small young spinach leaves*
*8 cherry tomatoes, halved*
*1 avocado, peeled, stoned and diced*
*2 oz (50 g) butter*
*grated rind and juice of 1 lemon*
*2 cloves garlic, crushed*
*4 tbsp chopped chives or spring onion tops*
*8 oz (225 g) small mushrooms*

Wash the spinach leaves thoroughly and pat dry. Arrange around the edge of a salad bowl with the tomatoes and avocado. Melt the butter and sauté the chives or spring onions, lemon rind and garlic for a few minutes. Add the mushrooms and cook for 5 minutes, stirring from time to time. Add the potatoes and toss until evenly coated. Place in the centre of the salad. Garnish with the shelled and quartered hard-boiled eggs. Stir the lemon juice into the pan juices and allow to come to the boil. Pour over the salad and serve immediately.

## TUNA AND SWEETCORN SALAD
Serves 4

*1 large tin tuna*
*12 oz (350 g) can sweetcorn, drained*
*3 spring onions, finely sliced*
*¼ pint (150 ml) soured cream*
*salt and freshly ground pepper*
*1 large red pepper*

In a large bowl mix together the soured cream, sweetcorn, spring onions, pepper and salt. Cut the stalk end from the red pepper and remove all the seeds and white pith. Slice into thin rings. Divide the tuna chunks equally between the individual plates and pile some of the sweetcorn salad on the side, together with a couple of rings of pepper. Sprinkle with chopped parsley.

## CRISPY PASTA COCKTAIL
Serves 6

*1½ oz (35 g) pasta wheels*
*1 crisp, red eating apple*
*2 sticks celery*
*1 firm tomato*

*Dressing;*
*4 tbsp good mayonnaise*
*1 tbsp tomato sauce*
*1 tbsp cream*
*2 tsp lemon juice*
*dash of Worcestershire or Tabasco sauce*

Cook the pasta in plenty of boiling, salted water until tender. Strain in a colander and place under running cold water for a few moments. Mix all the dressing ingredients together. Wash and slice the celery finely. Quarter and core the apple and cut into small dice. Cut the tomato in half and remove the seeds; cut the flesh into small dice. Mix the vegetables and pasta into the dressing and pile into glass dishes lined with lettuce leaves. Sprinkle with a little cayenne pepper and place a twist of lemon on top to decorate.

# CHERRY AND AVOCADO SALAD
Serves 4

*6 oz (175 g) sweet red or black cherries*
*2 small ripe avocados*
*2 tbsp chopped fresh mint*
*1 tbsp chopped fresh tarragon*
*3 tbsp olive oil*
*1 tbsp red wine vinegar*
*black pepper*
*1 small crisp lettuce*
*4 oz (110 g) curd cheese*

Stone the cherries. Peel and stone the avocados and cut them into cubes. Place both in a bowl with the mint and tarragon. In another bowl mix together the oil, vinegar and pepper to taste then fold the dressing into the cherries and avocados. Make a bed of lettuce on a serving dish and pile the salad mixture on top. Spoon over the curd cheese and serve immediately.

# INDEX